# WORTHINESS IS YOUR SUPERPOWER

The hidden link between knowing you're
worthy and living your truth

BY

Michelle Hollinger

Copyright 2025 Michelle Hollinger
All rights reserved

# DEDICATION

I dedicate this book to the younger versions of ourselves who thought they were unworthy but held it down the best way they could until we could discover the truth.

# TABLE OF CONTENTS

# INTRODUCTION

Some people are born into circumstances that allow them to hit the ground running. The circumstances of each person's life vary, but when the circumstances do not compromise authenticity and worthiness, the person is far more likely to create a wonderful, fulfilling, successful life they love. No life is perfect, but a life built on authenticity and worthiness creates a trajectory that is significantly more gratifying than not.

The rest of us were born into circumstances that thwarted our authenticity and wounded our perception of our worthiness. Contrary to popular opinion, regardless of the circumstances you were born into, you are meant to create a life you love. Your journey to that life will be different when authenticity and worthiness are not mainstays, but you are not meant to settle indefinitely. You are not meant to struggle forever. You're not meant to be stressed out more often than not, living for the weekend, constantly comparing yourself to others you think were dealt a better hand.

You were born to create your best life, a life that reflects you. The real you. The authentic you. The you that has been concealed by the circumstances of your life. The you that's been suppressed because its presence wasn't fully welcomed, appreciated and validated. The you beneath the unworthiness.

A critical aspect of the journey to your best life is getting to know *that* version of yourself. It's really the only way. A life built from anything other than your authentic self cannot be authentic, so how can it be your best life?

And get this. Peeling back the layers to discover who you really are introduces you to your innate worth. Getting to know the real you, understanding and appreciating each version of you from your birth to the present moment, helps you understand that while the circumstances you encountered impacted you, they do not define you.

You are meant to come face to face with the person you are without all the baggage and trauma and stuff that was piled on as you navigated the complexities of your life. When you do, there's a surreal energy that rises within you, clarifying, connecting dots and making it all make sense.

When you're able to see yourself clearly and understand why being the lesser versions of yourself was necessary to protect you until you could return to your authentic self, you create space for your authentic self to emerge; and with it, comes an alignment with your worthiness that shines a light on your path forward.

This book includes a roadmap back to your worth that includes the discovery of who you really are beneath the unworthiness. You get to immerse yourself into your worthiness, cultivate it, expand it, celebrate it and use it to create the life you love. It will help you remove the limitations that unworthiness plastered all over you through the various circumstances that impacted your worthiness without you realizing it.

You will be empowered from the inside-out. You will free up space for your worthiness and all the amazing qualities that make you who you are to expand, become normalized and ultimately, transform your life.

# CHAPTER 1

# AUTHENTICALLY WORTHY

Not knowing your authentic self invites unworthiness into the fold and allows it to become the guiding force creating a life that matches its low energy. Unworthiness is the culprit creating the distorted perceptions you have of yourself. Beliefs that you are not enough, that you cannot be loved, that you never get it right and are destined for a life that sucks flow from unworthiness.

The real you is none of those things. Your authentic self is enough. The qualities within it might be untapped, but they're there - waiting to be discovered, activated and put to good use. Qualities like courage, resilience, wisdom, power, faith, creativity and more exist within your authenticity and are activated by your worthiness.

That's why getting to know the real you **guarantees** you discover that you are worthy. Please allow that to sink in.

You're worthy simply because you exist. There's nothing you have to do to earn it. It's an inherent quality that arrived with you, in you, along with your authenticity. Both are determining factors in the quality of life. Both determine whether your life is spent plugged into and expressing the mission of your soul, or disconnected from it and searching for answers in all the wrong places. Both are underrated in conversations about living life to the fullest, despite the impossibility of living fully without them.

Getting to the nitty gritty of worthiness and authenticity requires becoming an archeologist of sorts in your own life. Going back, not to rehash, but to understand. Looking back with a wider lens that allows you to see the bigger picture. To take in dynamics invisible to you while you were in the thick of circumstances. To escape victimhood by depersonalizing experiences, taking back your power and standing in your truth.

In retrospect, you can discern the mask of unworthiness, with its invisible but powerful impact on your tendency to self-sabotage, procrastinate, talk yourself out of pursuing goals with your name on them. Unworthiness is the thread linking the survival skills and conditioned behavior you learned to navigate your childhood, to the limiting beliefs that plagued your adolescence and continue to shape your adulthood.

You are not alone. You are among the millions of people living with functional unworthiness. You are alive and mostly well, living an existence where you can pay your bills, keep a roof over your head, food on the table and clothes on your back, but truth be told, you're frustrated because you know you're meant to be, do and have more.

"I'm dealing with unworthiness," would probably NOT be the response you offer if someone asked you what's preventing you from thriving, but it's the right answer if you are going to a job you hate, tolerating toxic relationships, shrinking, settling, dimming your light. Unworthiness is the underlying factor if you are a people-pleaser, if you say "yes" when you want to say "no," if you deny yourself pleasure, go from drama to drama, from bad relationship to bad relationship, financial struggle to financial struggle. Unworthiness is all up in self-sabotage, imposter syndrome and the tendency to take a few steps forward, followed inevitably by the same number of steps backward.

Unworthiness is subtle, potentially lethal and difficult to identify because it's so pervasive. It's become more rampant with social media, which provides cover while exasperating the issue.

That you are holding this book means somewhere along your journey, your worthiness was smothered. Some situation convinced you that you were unworthy and unworthiness became a part of your personal belief system. At some point, you were taught to equate money, career, material possessions with your worthiness, so even if you're rolling in "success," there is still an inner emptiness you cannot explain. And because you've been taught that those external possessions define worthiness, the absence of them in your life is more confirmation that you are unworthy.

Unworthiness is a strong, but silent belief within the confines of your subconscious, secretly keeping you on the hamster wheel of life. It's an insidious, normalized aspect of your life that has room to flourish because you don't know it's there. Unworthiness keeps college educated people struggling from paycheck to paycheck. It keeps women in longterm, dysfunctional marriages. It's behind toxic masculinity and all of the "isms." At its most dangerous, unworthiness, combined with self-loathing and unbridled power inflicts harm on others. (See Donald Trump, Elon Musk, etc.)

Also dangerous, but used as an inwardly focused weapon, unworthiness on a personal scale creates a belief system steeped in self-imposed limitations that are difficult to resolve because they're difficult to spot. Learning how unworthiness functions, however, empowers you to identify it and dissolve it.

Unworthiness wreaks havoc because your brain is a goal seeking machine that looks for and finds experiences to support your belief. The experiences confirm your beliefs, ("see, I told you I couldn't do it,") which bring more experiences and the cycle of your life continues.

The good news about beliefs is that they can be changed. And the most important, foundational belief for you to change is that you're unworthy. Knowing you are worthy opens you up to a whole new way of being. It has existed within you since you were born, so your worthiness is available to you and reconnecting to it is completely within your power. It truly is your superpower, capable of manifesting more than you have ever imagined.

Knowing, embracing and living as your authentic self, awakens your innate worth. When you understand the dynamics of your life and why it was necessary for you to be lesser versions of yourself throughout every phase - from childhood, to your youth, to early adulthood, to where you are now - you can gain an understanding of how your worthiness and your authenticity intertwine.

Whenever unworthiness plays a dominant role in a person's life, inauthenticity is also at play.

To see clearly that you're worthy, it's necessary to understand what made you believe otherwise. It's necessary to examine how the factors in your life that clouded your view of your worthiness were simultaneously compelling you to suppress the real you. In order for you to subconsciously believe you were unworthy, you had to function as a distorted version of yourself created to exist in spaces where being the real you was unwelcome.

So people-pleasing, dimming your light, suppressing your thoughts and feelings, and denying your true self, are behaviors you were conditioned to exhibit in those spaces where you got pushback for being authentic. It makes sense. How is it possible to feel worthy when you feel compelled to be something other than what you are? Each time you found it necessary to be someone other than yourself, the message that was incorporated in your subconscious was, not only were you not worthy of being the real you, but that there was something wrong with that version.

That's the okie-doke that keeps you looking for solutions in all the wrong places - outside of yourself. The answer is within. It's in discovering who you really are. Accepting that there's nothing wrong with who you really are. And giving space for who you really are to emerge.

You are meant to create a life where feeling free to be YOU comes naturally. A life where your authentic self is in the driver's seat, unapologetically calling shots that align with the mission of your soul.

But in order to BE you, you must KNOW you. And the more you know you, the more you begin to realize that you are not what happened to you. You are not what people told you you are. You are not a mistake. You are not the circumstances that convinced you that you're unworthy.

You were born on purpose, with a purpose.

You were born worthy. You're worthy right now. And you will always be worthy.

Freeing yourself from others' opinions and expectations of who you are and how you're meant to live opens the pathway to knowing yourself *for* yourself and realizing that you are worthy of a life that allows you to do what you want, when you want, how you want. That might sound like an existence meant for other people because you've been convinced that it's unrealistic to even consider as much for yourself. But you're meant to do more than simply consider it. You are meant to embody it. Integrate it. Bask in it and allow it to be your foundation. You're meant to expect it to be a reality for you.

Without knowing who you really are and feeling worthy, what you're meant to be, do and have could end up in the cemetery with the gazillions of unwritten books, brilliant business ideas, innovative products and services that could change others' lives as well as your own. Not only that, the cemetery is full of un-lived lives. Lives that people were too afraid of embracing, scared to reveal because they did not feel worthy. These are the same people who lived lives to please others and ended up on their deathbed with a boat load of regrets.

Worthiness is that quality you didn't know you needed because it really doesn't get the attention it deserves. But it is the difference between settling for a life you think you should be satisfied with and a life that is a beautiful reflection of who you are. Worthiness is the unsung hero that holds the key to transforming virtually any area of your life that is not what you'd like it to be.

From money to relationships to health, to creatively expressing the gifts and talents with your name on them, your worthiness determines your experiences and what you're able to manifest.

## The Pervasiveness of Unworthiness

The powers that be want segments of society to believe that only certain people are worthy. That's complete hogwash. When people realize they're worthy, they become unstoppable and refuse to accept less than they deserve. Unsuccessful people assume that successful people living full, meaningful lives have something others do not. They don't.

The difference is that they're aware of it and live with the power and freedom it provides. But they're not announcing their worthiness to the world. They don't have to announce it because its energy oozes from their thoughts, words and actions. And truthfully, most successful people might not even realize that it's their worthiness that affords them access to their success. They just feel this insatiable urge to be, do and have experiences they refuse to allow anyone or anything to deny them. There's an inner knowingness about what they will become. The *how* might not be clear, but they are determined to get to the *what*. People who know they're worthy know who they are. Being their authentic self comes naturally. Worthiness is, ironically, authentic. It's not something that can be faked.

People who know they're worthy have a worth consciousness that informs how they see themselves, how they see others and how they see the world. They move differently and organically avoid obstacles people under the spell of unworthiness routinely bump up against. Because worthiness and unworthiness are essentially states of consciousness, the energy flowing from either manifests lives that align with one or the other.

People who know they're worthy tend to focus on what they want, not what they don't want because unworthiness isn't blocking their view of who they really are. They do not fall prey to the powers that be that want you to feel unworthy if you have a certain skin color, are a certain gender, love certain people, come from certain zip codes and other external qualities that have nothing to do with your worthiness. The truth is you were born worthy, you're worthy right now and you will always be worthy, but if you don't feel worthy, you're far more likely to fall under the spell of so-called leaders, whose agenda is strengthened by your unworthiness.

You cannot manifest beyond a certain mental set point established by the level of your worthiness. Although the level was probably established based on your interactions with others who did not know better, it is a self-fulfilling limitation you and only you can raise.

Your worthiness is far more powerful than you realize but you have to remove the gunk preventing your direct access to it. You can remove the gunk by changing the way you think, infusing your life with gratitude, forgiving folk, clarifying whether your religious beliefs are keeping you stuck, checking out your relationship with money, embracing peace and being intentional about your worthiness. Worthiness is also a powerful tool for releasing trauma, another thick, dense barrier to your authenticity.

Without awakening your worthiness and your authenticity, you can live your entire life coming nowhere near a life you love because unworthiness blocks you from the best parts of you, the real you.

And it's frustrating because you have no idea that unworthiness is the invisible monkey wrench flipping your best laid plans on their head. It's especially aggravating when you're doing your best and can't figure out what's stopping you. You're learning new things and putting them into action, but still taking two steps forward and two giant steps back.

Unworthiness is like carbon monoxide, it's invisible and potentially lethal because if you don't know it's there, there's nothing you can do about it as it slowly sucks the life out of you. Millions of people are battling unworthiness without even realizing it because you don't have to be dealing with a chronic condition for it to exist. You don't have to be down and out.

In fact, it is most effective in lives that look good from the outside looking in. When your life looks socially acceptable, unworthiness can run rampant because it normalizes the lies you tell yourself about why you can't achieve your dreams. And when you're not aware that it's unworthiness that's preventing you from creating the life you love, it's easier to blame people, circumstances, your past, the world and all its limitations. But all that does is keep you feeling powerless because you assume the solution is outside of you. You believe that in order for your life to improve, the powers that be must create better circumstances when the real solution exists within you. It's your worthiness and it is your superpower.

# HOME

By Samuel Crowe / Sophie Peterson Bond
Performed by Iyamah

Yeah
Home, it don't have to be a physical place
Or a familiar face, somewhere that you feel safe
And can escape, when you wanna be alone
Uh, home, yeah

You can find it wherever you are, oh
When we sit with the birds
Nature or nurture is heard
Yeah, it's bigger than us, you belong to me

And I think 'bout the girl
All she wanted was to save the world
But it's got to start within, and now I'm home
Got the keys to my own door

And I take them where I go
Oh oh, I set the tone, I set the code for home
I got the keys to my own door
And I take them where I go, oh
I set the tone, and the code for home
Home, home
But still, I'm searching for -

All she wanted was somewhere she could call home
But when time's up, you can't stay, you must move on
Start again, hey, I know how it feels (ooh)
When you feel nothing but fear

Know that you can still break free, yeah
Uh, scared, I thought no one cared
I had to be the best thing for me
And oh, when I sit with the birds
I realize it's bigger than me, it's bigger than us
It's bigger than what we could ever see

So I keep up the love and the mother in me
Try to keep an open mind and my heart on my sleeve
Oh, I'd almost gave up if you know what I mean
So I had to slow down, feel the ground beneath my feet
Take me back to when I was, I was 17, yeah
And tell my younger self to hold on to her dreams

Cause now I'm home
Got the keys to my own door
And I take them where I go
Oh oh, I set the tone, I set the code for home

I got the keys to my own door
And I take them where I go
Oh, I set the tone, and the code for home
Home, home

Oh, and still, I am searching for

Security and honesty
The balance of it all and everything

I want to free all of my forgotten dreams
I lost it all so suddenly

Oh yeah, oh yeah, oh yeah baby
Structure, stability it's
Bigger than the eyes can see

CHAPTER 2

# THE ORIGINS
# OF UNWORTHINESS

So, if it's true that you were born worthy, you're worthy right now and will always be worthy, where does unworthiness come from? It's first important to understand that unworthiness is a flawed perspective that is not based in truth.

Unworthiness typically stems from childhood experiences, societal conditioning and repeated messages that made you question your inherent value. Because it operates beneath the surface, quietly shaping how you see yourself, you probably had no idea it was even there, becoming so ingrained that it felt like it was a part of your personality. It's actually a belief system that grew as you did, widening the distance between you and your worthiness.

The childhood experiences run the gamut from traumas like abandonment or abuse to a situational event like an exhausted parent who said something hurtful when you needed their love and attention. Whatever the harmful experience, it makes sense for a young mind to assume that they deserved it or that it somehow means something about them in terms of not being lovable or worthy of better circumstances.

Feeling defined by their circumstances wreaks havoc on young minds that naturally trust the caretakers in their life to take good care of them. It is the most deeply entrenched source of unworthiness because it goes to the core of a person's self-perception, creating a mental framework that gets internalized and functions as the foundational belief system.

The family you were born into and whether they knew they were worthy plays a big role in the dynamics you experienced. Parents living authentically with their worthiness intact tend to create spaces for their children's worthiness to thrive. Parents who are struggling through their own bouts of unworthiness typically do not have the self-agency or the mental and emotional tools necessary to cultivate their child's connection to their own worthiness.

The way you're treated by people who are responsible for you (including teachers, preachers, coaches, etc.) tells you who they think you are, which informs who you think you are. Left unhealed and unresolved, that thought process morphs into a general feeling of unspoken unworthiness, which becomes a core belief that your subconscious mind obeys by finding matching experiences.

You subconsciously found reinforcement of your limited belief and next thing you know, you're an adult going to a job you hate, tolerating unhealthy relationships, dimming your light, people-pleasing, being ruled by fear, romanticizing mediocrity and struggling when you're actually capable of so much more. Unworthiness distorts who you really are - a spiritual being having this human experience with the power to create a life that provides far more goodness than the one you're currently living.

The great news is that your worthiness is waiting for you and can be instrumental to you healing the unresolved beliefs that led to unworthiness taking root in your subconsciousness. While it might have been smothered beneath harmful experiences, your worthiness came here with you when you arrived on the planet. It is the key that unlocks the treasure chest of goodness within, full of strength, wisdom, creativity, peace, resilience, joy, authentic power and everything you need to live the life meant for you.

Unworthiness guards the entrance to the treasure chest, keeping you disconnected from life-changing qualities that you've used here and there when your back was against the wall or when you were in a pinch. You're not sure they exist within you because that's how effective unworthiness is - it has you doubting who you really are and what you're made of.

But these qualities are meant to be used intentionally. They're meant to be regular mainstays that you use to create and savor a life you love. Your worthiness is available to you and reconnecting to it is simpler than you think. It truly is your superpower because when you become curious about where it leads, the possibilities are endless.

# SWEET FREEDOM

By Rodney Lynn Temperton
Performed by Michael McDonald

No more runnin' down the wrong road
Dancin' to a diff'rent drum
Can't you see what's goin' on
Deep inside your heart

Always searchin' for the real thing
Livin' like it's far away
Just leave all the madness in yesterday
You're holdin' the key
When you believe it

Shine sweet freedom
Shine your light on me
You are the magic
You're right where I wanna be

Oh sweet freedom carry me along
We'll keep the spirit alive on and on
Oh-oh-oh

We'll be dancin' in the moonlight
Smilin' with the risin' sun
Livin' like we've never done
Goin' all the way (go)

Reachin' out to meet the changes
Touchin' every shining star
The light of tomorrow is right where we are
There's no turnin' back
From what I'm feeling

Shine sweet freedom
Shine your light on me
You are the magic
You're right where I wanna be

Oh sweet freedom carry me along
We'll keep the spirit alive on and on
Hoo-oh-oh-oh

'Cause there'll be starlight all night
When we're close together
Share those feelings dancin' in your eyes tonight
They're guiding us
Shinin' till the mornin' light

Oh-oh-oh
Shine sweet freedom
Shine your light on me
You are the magic
You're right where I wanna be

Oh sweet freedom carry me along
We'll keep the spirit alive on and on
Shine sweet freedom

Shine your light on me
You are the magic
Magic baby

Oh sweet freedom carry me along
Come on, on and on
Shine sweet freedom
Shine your light on me
On and on, on and on, on and on
Oh sweet freedom carry me along
We'll keep the spirit alive on and on, oh

# CHAPTER 3

# THINK WORTHY THOUGHTS

The life you're living right now is a result of how you think and a direct reflection of what you feel worthy of having. Take a deep breath.

Whether you're living a harmonious, joyful life with occasional challenges you face and overcome; or you're constantly struggling to manifest better circumstances, or your life fits somewhere between those two dynamics, the level of worthiness you feel is the determining factor. If unworthiness exists in your consciousness, the thoughts you think keep it alive, essentially limiting you from creating the life you love.

The danger of unworthiness is its subtlety. It operates beneath the surface of your life and shapes the way you think about yourself, your life and what you believe it can be. Unworthiness restricts you in ways you're not even aware of because of how low-key it operates. Even if you're living what

- from the outside looking in - looks like a "good" life, if it emerged from a sense of unworthiness, it's limiting because it's blocking you from being YOU.

If you can accept that, there's more for you to consider because life does not happen *to* you, life happens *through* you. The powers that be, your parents, the economy, your hubby, the man, nothing outside of you is responsible for your life. Those entities are bit players doing their part to play out the drama as it unfolds, but you are the director and your thoughts are the script. The quality of your script is determined by how worthy you feel.

Interestingly, those bit players typically play a humongous role in your relationship with your authenticity. Chances are, the messages you received from them, verbally and nonverbally, convinced you to engage in survival skills to feel safe in their presence. Survival skills like people-pleasing, dimming your light, suppressing your real thoughts and feelings, and essentially pretending to be someone you were not because you did not feel free to be your authentic self.

Reflect on your thought process as you engaged in survival skills and you will probably draw a blank. That's because you were not functioning from your prefrontal cortex, the part of your brain that makes conscious decisions. You were functioning from your amygdala, the part of the brain that's activated when you're feeling fearful.

If you *could* recall your thoughts, they might have been something along the lines of, "I really need them to like me, so I'm not going to speak up and say something that disagrees with them." Or, "I do not want to chance being rejected by my parents, so even though I'm not interested in _________ and would really prefer to be doing _________, I'm going to keep my feelings to myself." Or, "Whenever I talk about how great I'm doing at work, my boyfriend's eyes glaze over and he changes the subject, so I'm going to tone things down on the job." Or, "I really want to major in English Literature and become a writer but my mother expects me to become a lawyer like her, so I'm going to law school instead."

The thoughts that supported the conditioned behavior, which became habitual and felt like a part of your personality, were functioning without your knowledge. They became a part of your subconscious mind, where your memories, beliefs and values are stored. Those same thoughts became the basis for how you lived your life, how you saw yourself, what you believed about yourself and ultimately, how you made decisions.

Your conditioned behavior is a basis for much of your thinking, but not all of it. Generational patterns, family dynamics, societal standards and prevailing ways of being impact you and the way you think far more than you realize.

But understanding the source of your thinking helps you discern whether your thoughts have merit. Understanding their source and validity is imperative to taking control of what you think.

When you consider that humans think an average of 60,000 thoughts each day, it really emphasizes the importance of taking control of your mental activity. When you consider that 90 percent of thoughts are repetitive and 80 percent are negative, it's really no wonder so many people are merely going through the motions of living, settling for mediocrity because they don't realize the power their thoughts contain.

Venice Bloodworth sums up the power of our thinking in her book *Key to Yourself.* "Thinking is the true business of life. Thinkers rule the world They always have and they always will. All people think, but the tragedy of life is that so few of us think creatively or constructively; so few recognize the fact that thought is a creative force.

We live in the same world and are as far apart as the difference in our thought processes. Some fail while others succeed; some are sick, others are healthy; some are miserable, others happy. We all want to blame luck or fate or some one of our fellow men but the difference is within ourselves. We are the product of our prevailing habits of thought."

Ultimately, this goes beyond positive thinking. You can transform your thoughts and your thoughts can reconnect you to your innate worth. You might not be aware of what your thoughts are, but the circumstances throughout your day reveal to you how you think. Real life scenarios show you - in real time

- the predominant pattern of your thinking because what you think about, you bring about.

If you're frequently sick, what are your thoughts about health? If you're struggling financially, what money thoughts run through your mind day in and day out? If your relationships are stressful, what do you think about how people should get along?

To make it even more practical, if you go to work rehearsing what you'll say to that co-worker who knows how to push all of your buttons, you are essentially guaranteeing that you and that co-worker will bump heads. If you picture yourself cussing out the next person who says something you don't like, you're telling your subconscious mind to bring you somebody to cuss out. If you haven't gone on a date in years because there are no good prospects out there, you will have experiences that confirm to you that absence of good prospects (among the billions of people on the planet.)

In each of these scenarios, your thoughts have created experiences that you do not want, that you complain about and that you subconsciously keep alive because of your thoughts. And they're flowing from a space of unworthiness that prevents you from seeing how powerful you actually are.

You are thinking negatively without even realizing it. You might even believe you're thinking positively. Always considering the worst case scenario feels productive, and it is, but not in the way you want. Technically it is productive because it produces a matching result – but it's not what you say you want. By thinking about what you would do in a worse case scenario, you attract the worst case into your life every time. And because you were prepared for it, you feel like you've accomplished something important since you're able to navigate it.

But think about it. By always preparing for worst case scenarios, you're stringing together a life of worst case scenarios. It's like you're tricking yourself into struggling because you believe that by rehearsing what you'll do when things go wrong, you're "adulting."

But what you're actually doing is maintaining stressful, frustrating circumstances because of the way you think about them. Because many of us were unwittingly raised to think negatively, it feels like you're being productive by exploring what could go wrong. It seems like the responsible thing to do is to have something to fall back on when things don't work out.

You believe you're being realistic by mapping out how your plans could go awry; you say you're being responsible by being prepared for the crazy outcomes before they come. You think you're protecting yourself by bracing for "the other shoe to drop."

But here's the thing, thoughts held in mind, produce after their kind in EVERY situation. In other words, every experience you have originated with a thought. That's the way spiritual law works and we're all using it whether we're aware of it or not.

And because you're not just *thinking* about the poor result but also picturing it and mentally preparing for it - it actually manifests.

Experiencing the negative situation confirms one of your negative beliefs, like "if it's not one thing, it's another," or "if anything can go wrong, it will," or "if it wasn't for bad luck, I would have no luck at all," "I can't win for losing," or "when it rains, it pours," - creating a cycle of negativity that continues to feed your negative thoughts, which manifest as negative experiences, and so forth and so on.

Having a predominantly negative pattern of thinking typically extends itself into other behaviors. Do you gossip, criticize and complain often? Are you known for your sarcastic, snarky remarks? You're basically tossing out a boomerang of negativity that's bringing you matching experiences.

The beautiful thing about your thoughts is that they're completely changeable. If you're dissatisfied with what you're experiencing, you have the power to change it, but not by changing anything externally. To approach it that way gets you a different set of circumstances that are temporary at best, but eventually the negative thoughts you're still thinking will bring you experiences that match their energy.

Plus, expecting other people or situations to change in order for you to feel better is giving up all your power. What if the other people or situations never change? What if they can't?

You change your life by first changing your thoughts so that you are thinking about what you *do* want, not what you don't. If you don't understand how your subconscious mind functions, it can trip you up. Your subconscious mind pays attention to the thought itself and operates as though you only think about what you're interested in manifesting.

For example, you think about how you do not want to be broke. How you do not want to get into another argument. How you do not want to catch the flu. How you're tired of being stuck in the same position. All your subconscious mind pays attention to in those thought processes are the things you describe. Being broke. Another argument. Catching the flu. Stuck in the same position. And it goes to work manifesting those outcomes. Your subconscious assumes you're interested in what you think about so it makes sure you keep having the same types of experiences.

Thinking about what you *want* changes those thoughts from "I don't want to be broke" to "I expect to have money." From "I don't want to get into another argument" to "I am open to a peaceful relationship." From "I don't want to catch the flu" to "I am healthy and strong" From "I'm tired of being stuck in this position" to "I'm ready to being promoted." See the difference?

Where did your negative thoughts come from and what keeps them going? Most, if not all, have their basis in childhood experiences where you learned conditioned behaviors like shrinking, people-pleasing, suppressing true feelings, dimming your light and denying your authenticity.

These behaviors reinforced a subconscious belief that you were unworthy and unworthiness functions with your untrained ego, which is responsible for keeping you safe. To your untrained ego, safe means familiar, "comfort zone," action, limited to what you already know, what you've already experienced, whether it serves you or not.

When your subconscious is full of memories and experiences that require you to be something other than who you really are by suppressing your truth, people-pleasing, etc., you think thoughts that support the maintenance of those behaviors. The only way to change your thoughts is to first become aware of what you're thinking.

Every experience in your life has an invisible tether to an originating thought. If you're having financial problems, follow the tether to your thoughts to reveal what you say to yourself about money and the inevitably of not having enough. If you're constantly dealing with health challenges, follow the tether to your beliefs about sickness being way of life, inherited and a random roll of the dice. If you're navigating toxic relationships, follow the tether to your thoughts about how you deserve to be treated.

Unworthiness is the undercurrent of negative thinking. Shifting your perception of your worthiness awakens your ability to take control of your thinking. It's an inside-out process that requires more than simply thinking positively. Changing your thoughts without dissolving unworthiness is a temporary

Band-aid approach that does nothing to permanently shift the dynamics of your life.

Cultivating the fundamental belief that you were born worthy, you're worthy right now and will always be worthy regardless of any circumstances is the starting point for unraveling the tether to your negative thoughts and forging a new tether rooted in your worthiness.

# WE CLOSE OUR EYES

By Peter Cox and Richard Drummie
Performed by Go West

Inside, everyone hides one desire
Outside, no one would know
Danger, close to the edge of the knife
Safer not to let go
And while we miss chances
You can almost hear time slipping away

We close our eyes, we never lose a game
Imagination never lets us take the blame
We close our eyes to see the final frame
We close our eyes to time slipping away

No show, Wednesday girl waits with the wine
She knows just what to say
While no one listens
You can almost hear time slipping away

We close our eyes, we never lose a game
Imagination never lets us take the blame
We close our eyes to see the final frame
We close our eyes and
We can talk to strangers
We are burning with the spark

And we can walk on water
We are tigers in the dark
We are burning
We close our eyes

Heroes never give in to the night
He knows how far he can run
And as he surrenders
You can almost hear time slipping away

We close our eyes, we never lose a game
Imagination never lets us take the blame
We close our eyes to see the final frame
We close our eyes
We close our eyes, we never lose a game
Imagination never lets us take the blame
We close our eyes to see the final frame
We close our eyes
We close our eyes, we walk on water
Lets us take the blame
We are burning

CHAPTER 4

# WORTHY AND FORGIVEN (SELF-FORGIVENESS)

Forgiveness is a non-negotiable part of your journey to create a life you love, a life based on your worthiness and authenticity. Forgiveness allows you to transmute negative energy into energy you can use to manifest what you're here to be, do and have. Activating your worthiness equips you with the wisdom required for forgiveness because it allows you to see beyond victimhood. It's a natural progression from awakening your worthiness, realizing the power of your thoughts and walking the path of forgiveness.

The worthier you feel, the more inclined you are to see the bigger picture. The more you embody your authenticity, the more you realize how others operated from their inauthenticity and their unworthiness. Seeing your own journey clearly helps you better understand others.

Worthiness empowers you to think from different perspectives, like being able to understand that "hurt people, hurt people." Knowing you're worthy helps you see what has harmed you from a different perspective. It helps you understand that how you think about past hurts can keep you hostage to them. It helps you see how not forgiving maintains your membership in club victimhood.

The most important forgiving you will ever do begins with forgiving yourself - every iteration of you, from the time you were born to the person you are now. It's essential to revisit aspects of yourself that you judge and condemn and wish she/he had been different, better, stronger, more. Self-forgiveness frees you to see yourself accurately.

Forgiving previous versions of yourself allows you clear access to your worthiness and authenticity. As long as you judge or condemn parts of yourself, the energy of unworthiness is active and controlling you without your awareness or permission. Your belief that those versions of you were unworthy is woven throughout your judgement, keeping unworthiness alive and well within you. It perpetuates a vicious cycle of unworthiness since the present version of you can never fully embody worthiness if you believe any version of you was ever unworthy.

You were born worthy, you have always been worthy, you're worthy right now and you will always be worthy. No circumstance defines your worthiness. Take a deep breath.

Your worthiness isn't the only thing taking a hit when you don't forgive. Your authenticity is impacted, too. Without forgiving yourself, the disconnect between who you are now and your authentic self grows wider. Judgment feels like an attack so it protects your authenticity by becoming a stronger barrier. Your authenticity has a breath all its own, but it needs space within you to inhale and exhale. It needs space to unfold. Space to be. Forgiving yourself creates space.

Self-forgiveness is a powerful process that is the gateway to your freedom. It's the ingredient necessary for having an intimate connection to your worthiness and taking a deep, expansive dive into your authenticity. Done effectively, forgiving leads to understanding, and when you fully understand who you were and why, you can feel grateful that he/she existed the way they did. Forgiving provides the revelation that you couldn't be who you are now without them.

Even if you're not actively thinking about younger versions of yourself you wish had been different, your subconscious mind holds the judgment and the energy is impacting your current reality. Ultimately, you will know you fully understand the younger versions of yourself when audacious thankfulness flows to the surface.

# Four Step Self-Forgiveness Process

The process of self-forgiveness requires forgiving every version of yourself that you judge - especially versions you feel any degree of shame or guilt around. Forgiving past versions of yourself is important because your subconscious mind, which is the storehouse of your memories, beliefs and values, uses its content to manifest the experiences of your current life.

Without processing previous versions of yourself, the dynamics continue running your life without your awareness or consent. That means you can have an intellectual understanding and a conscious desire for a specific outcome, but if your subconscious has memories that run counter to your desire, the memories will win every time.

The first step is to forgive that version of yourself, (or to at least be *willing* to forgive if you're not quite ready.) You can move on to the second step with either because the next part includes understanding who you were at the time and becoming mindful of the dynamics at play in your life. (The second step actually deepens the first, and if done effectively, could help you appreciate that version so deeply that forgiving them is no longer necessary.)

My own personal example involves using the four step forgiveness process to shift from resentment and disappointment, to the deepest love and appreciation possible for a younger Michelle who made one of the biggest decisions of her life before she was ready to make it.

In the latter part of 2024, I was still processing the spiritual breakthrough (that felt like a nervous breakdown at the time) that brought me face to face with 22-year old Michelle. She was a senior at Florida State University and planning a June wedding to her high school sweetheart/boyfriend of five-years despite the onslaught of red flags clearly proclaiming neither of them ready for marriage.

But she was in love and certain he'd do better after they wed, so on June 29, 1985, Michelle and Morgan began an unhealthy alliance that would produce three beautiful children and last 26 years before she decided to call it quits.

My modern day turmoil ensued when I became thoroughly convinced that 22-year old Michelle *should* have known *then* what 61-year old Michelle knows *now*. Swimming in a thick coulda, woulda, shoulda stew, I spent at least an hour or so giving my younger self a smack down for choosing to become a wife at such a tender age.

*If only I'd opened my eyes. If only I'd discovered meditation sooner. If only I'd had people in my life who, if only, if only, if only*…. I was locked in, rehashing, regretting and fantasizing about the alternate reality I was certain younger Michelle would have enjoyed *if only* she had chosen differently.

I had no idea how much I resented her for being so gullible. I did not know how disappointed I was that she, a really smart person, was not smart enough to at least check in with her gut, which was surely screaming at the top of its lungs "don't do it!"

I had no idea how much I'd suppressed my true feelings about this immature version of myself and that those unresolved emotions were blocking me from loving the current and much improved version of Michelle.

The resentment and disappointment shocked me into tears. Always a strong indication that I had work to do, I put on my archeologist hat and began poking around 22-year old Michelle's consciousness to understand who she was and what led her to this monumental decision before she was ready to make it.

It didn't take long for me to realize that her childhood of trauma, loss and the absence of a "normal" family had her convinced that getting married would fill the empty spots her heart didn't know how to soothe. I began to understand why 22-year old Michelle was certain that becoming a wife and subsequently, a mother, would afford her the chance to experience the family life she missed out on because the people in her childhood were dying, abusive, absent or oblivious.

She was longing for safety and security and saw marrying a young man from a solid, two parent household, with three cool older brothers and an extended family headed by beautiful grandparents who hosted big holiday dinners and took family vacations as her ticket to normalcy. Immersed in meditative reflection with my closed eyes brimming with tears, I was seeing

22-year old Michelle for the first time and with each layer I peeled back, the more I respected her decision.

That newfound understanding gradually morphed into audacious thankfulness that this young girl was wise enough to choose the life she believed she needed. I was also thoroughly convinced she did the absolute best she could with what she knew. Sure, there was much she didn't know, but more importantly, I was able to acknowledge that my healed, trauma-free, significantly wiser 61-year self had no right to judge her for not knowing what she did not know.

Now, from a place of genuine gratitude, I could thank 22-year old Michelle. I could appreciate that not only was she doing what she thought was best for herself, but that she was also subconsciously doing what she thought was best for future versions of herself - which includes me! Then I realized that if she had not made the decisions she made, I would not be the woman I am today.

When I was able to understand her from this new perspective, a weight lifted from my shoulders and my emotions shifted so profoundly that I felt joy in the space that once held disappointment, appreciation instead of resentment. The energy reverberating through me felt different. There was a lightness I'd never known. Now completely overcome with emotion, I wondered why I even needed to forgive 22-year old Michelle because it was now so clear that she did nothing wrong!

Wait! If that worked so well for that beautiful young bride, I told myself, let me do the same thing for every version of myself that I was still judging. So I spent the next few hours using the four step process for every version of myself I felt any degree of regret, shame or guilt about. As I immersed myself into the process, I found myself moving from forgiveness to understanding to gratitude to a self-love more palpable and exhilarating than I ever imagined possible.

I did the work to realize that I'm worthy several years ago, but that realization went even deeper with this level of self-forgiveness. I know myself like I've never known me before and my authenticity feels safe to BE all that it is.

The self-forgiveness process will take you to new depths and awaken parts of yourself you might not know existed.

The four steps in the forgiveness process are:

1. **Forgiveness:** Choose a version of yourself you still judge. A time when you did or didn't do something you now wish you had or had not. Choose a version of yourself that conjures up disappointment or shame or guilt or an emotion that fuels regret and coulda, woulda, shoulda dynamics.

2. **Understanding:** Examine who he/she was. Think about what was going on in their life at the time. What went on prior to that time? Do your best to look at the bigger picture of their life to gain a deeper understanding of

who they were and why they were that way. Try to be as objective as possible. Consider the people in their life and what it was like engaging with them. Really look at the version of yourself like you would a younger cousin or dear friend. Bring compassion to the equation and cut yourself some much needed slack. What are you grateful for about that version of yourself? What was the underlying need that wasn't readily apparent back then? Can you see that he/she did the best they could with what they knew? Can you see that what you know now was not what they knew then? Can you understand their decision now?

3. **Audacious Thankfulness:** Now that you've had a chance to process the dynamics that were at play back then, do you feel grateful for that version of yourself? If not, are you willing to be grateful for that version of yourself? Can you accept that if they had not done what why did, you would not be who you are now - engaged in self-discovery work to reclaim your worthiness and authenticity? Can you see a brighter future for yourself because of the changed perception you have about your younger self?

4. **Self-Love:** This stage and the audacious thankfulness stage are not outcomes you work at. They are destinations that emerge when you've done the work to

forgive and understand, so repeat steps one and two as much as necessary. Depending on what you're attempting to forgive and understand, it might take more time. You and your younger self deserve to take as long as you need to process your experience and arrive at this deeply gratifying result of loving yourself deeper than you imagined possible.

*P.S. My ex-hubby and I are now dating. At 62, we are different versions of ourselves, healed and healing, far more emotionally mature, and capable of loving ourselves and, therefore, each other in ways a healthy relationship requires. We don't know what the future holds, but we're open the possibilities.*

# UNWRITTEN

Danielle A. Brisebois / Natasha Anne Bedingfield
/ Wayne Steven Jr Rodrigues
Performed by Natasha Bedingfield

I am unwritten
Can't read my mind
I'm undefined
I'm just beginning
The pen's in my hand
Ending unplanned

Staring at the blank page before you
Open up the dirty window
Let the sun illuminate the words that you could not find

Reaching for something in the distance
So close you can almost taste it
Release your inhibitions
Feel the rain on your skin
No one else can feel it for you
Only you can let it in
No one else, no one else
Can speak the words on your lips

Drench yourself in words unspoken
Live your life with arms wide open
Today is where your book begins
The rest is still unwritten
Oh, oh, oh

## Worthiness Is Your Superpower

I break tradition
Sometimes my tries are outside the lines
We've been conditioned to not make mistakes
But I can't live that way

Staring at the blank page before you
Open up the dirty window
Let the sun illuminate the words that you could not find
Reaching for something in the distance
So close you can almost taste it
Release your inhibitions
Feel the rain on your skin
No one else can feel it for you
Only you can let it in
No one else, no one else
Can speak the words on your lips

Drench yourself in words unspoken
Live your life with arms wide open
Today is where your book begins

Feel the rain on your skin
No one else can feel it for you
Only you can let it in
No one else, no one else
Can speak the words on your lips

Drench yourself in words unspoken
Live your life with arms wide open
Today is where your book begins
The rest is still unwritten

Staring at the blank page before you
Open up the dirty window
Let the sun illuminate the words that you could not find
Reaching for something in the distance
So close you can almost taste it

Release your inhibitions
Feel the rain on your skin
No one else can feel it for you
Only you can let it in
No one else, no one else
Can speak the words on your lips

Drench yourself in words unspoken
Live your life with arms wide open
Today is where your book begins
Feel the rain on your skin
No one else can feel it for you
Only you can let it in
No one else, no one else
Can speak the words on your lips

Drench yourself in words unspoken
Live your life with arms wide open
Today is where your book begins
The rest is still unwritten
The rest is still unwritten
The rest is still unwritten
Oh, yeah, yeah

50

CHAPTER 5

# WORTHY TO FORGIVE
## (Forgiving Others)

Self-forgiveness does a beautiful job of deepening the activation of your innate worth. From that vantage point, it becomes easier to see when others are not aware of theirs, providing understanding that makes forgiving them possible. When it comes to forgiving others, your worthiness empowers you to forgive. It lets you know you can survive the process because of who you really are and what you're really made of.

Forgiving frees you. That doesn't mean you condone the experiences or that you must befriend the person responsible for them. Ultimately, it means you're no longer willing to be chained to the experience. The forgiveness is for you. Forgiveness sets you free. Forgiveness transforms you from being a victim to reclaiming your power. The correlation between your worthiness and ability to forgive is packed with insight.

51

When you are able to examine how unworthiness shaped you, it's easier to see it at play in others' lives, as well. It's easier to see that their harmful behavior came from their own unworthiness and unhealed issues and, although you were on the receiving end of it, it wasn't actually about you.

That's one of the reasons it's actually not advised to include the person you're forgiving in your forgiveness process. Their perspective and yours might be completely different. How they see things has nothing to do with what you experienced, so making their agreement or understanding a part of you being able to forgive could stall your efforts. Forgiveness is for YOU. That being said, as you move into forgiveness, it's important for you to understand what it is and what it's not.

The forgiveness that is necessary for living your best life is not the wimpy "I can forgive, but I can't forget," stuff. And it does not involve revenge or payback or "killing them with kindness." The type of forgiveness required for living your best life is radical forgiveness and it goes far beyond what you might understand about "traditional" forgiveness, which is lip service without actual healing. The kind of forgiveness that is done to exact revenge or to "show them," isn't forgiveness at all. It's mind games that allow you to hold on to the experience while deluding yourself into believing that you have actually forgiven somebody.

When you "forgive" like that, you've got the incident in your back pocket waiting for the perfect opportunity to use it.

To free yourself and create a life you love, it's necessary for you to engage in the highest level of forgiveness possible. That's radical forgiveness. We're talking mature, life-changing, soul aligned grown folk stuff.

Radical forgiveness is deeply spiritual and heals unresolved issues that show up as seemingly immovable obstacles or recurring patterns until you recognize what is occurring. More often than not, the unresolved issue stems from a childhood experience that tender minds comprehended in a way that made sense to a child's level of understanding. Its emotional impact gets stored in a child's subconscious, remains there and because of the way our subconscious mind and our brains work, it eventually attracts unpleasant, sometimes painful experiences in adulthood that correlate to the unresolved childhood issue.

Of course, you are unlikely to consciously recognize the correlation. That's where radical forgiveness comes in. I was introduced to this process years ago during my training to become a spiritual prayer chaplain. We used the book, *Radical Forgiveness* by Colin Tipping, which is amazing. In it, he provides a really compelling example to illustrate just how radical forgiveness works. Tipping shares the story of his sister Julie's unraveling marriage and how showing her the correlation between the issues with her husband and unresolved issues with their father, helped her to heal and save her marriage.

Growing up, Julie was apparently starving for her father's affection, which he was not prone to share. She eventually convinced herself that because her dad was simply not an affectionate man, she would accept him as he was and stop expecting him to be affectionate with her. While her logical mind rationalized this dynamic between her and her father, subconsciously, she interpreted his lack of affection as rejection, that he didn't love her and that she was therefore unlovable. She tucked those hurt feelings away, believing she had survived this hurtful period by shutting down her expectations.

Years later, when she saw her father being affectionate with her young niece, Julie was surprised at how hurt she felt. And she had no idea that her unresolved sadness was the underlying reason most of her relationships were with men who did not show her the affection she craved.

Because unresolved daddy/daughter issues typically follow us into adulthood, it's no surprise Julie married a man seemingly incapable of showing affection. Like her father, her husband did not show affection and Julie convinced herself that he was incapable of doing so. She'd accepted that her marriage lacked the kind of loving physical gestures she craved and Julie learned to stop expecting it from her husband.

That was how she coped, until her stepdaughter was involved in a car accident and Julie's husband shattered her ideas about his inability to show affection when he lovingly doted on his daughter during her recovery. Livid. Seeing her husband be affectionate with his daughter drove Julie crazy and stirred up old feelings of insecurity and rejection she'd buried.

She resented her husband and he responded by resenting her right back because her behavior and energy towards him turned so inexplicably sour he couldn't take it.

They were on the brink of divorce when she visited her brother and he picked up on her sadness. After prodding a bit, he got her to open up about what was going on in her marriage. He listened intently before eventually asking her if she was willing to try a different approach. She reluctantly agreed, feeling like there was nothing he could say to help her but also like she had nothing to lose. Colin probed and got her to open up about the first time in her life she felt rejected because a man was not affectionate towards her. It was, of course, her father and all the memories she had of him not showing her affection came flooding back. Julie recalled how she accepted he couldn't be affectionate, but felt shattered when she discovered, years later, that he could.

She'd felt ashamed because, as an adult, the childhood anguish she thought she'd tucked deeply enough away reappeared in full force. When she fessed up to her brother, she fully expected him to laugh at her for acting childish when she was triggered by her father's display of affection to the young relative. Not only did he not laugh, he told her it was a great indication that what she was experiencing could be resolved if she was willing to open her mind to what he was about to suggest.

He explained that the reason her husband's behavior around affection bothered her so much was because her soul and her husband's soul had conspired for the healing opportunity her marriage presented her – if she was willing to see it. He explained that the trouble she had in her marriage was correlated to the unresolved, unhealed issues she'd had with her father and his seeming inability to display affection towards her. Colin helped her to see that because she had this deep internal hurt that fostered a sense of unworthiness, she unwittingly and unconsciously attracted relationships that presented her with the same issue, not to punish her but to afford her an opportunity to heal.

If she was willing and able to see the correlation, she could do the work necessary to heal the childhood hurt – which he explained would free her from the angst she was experiencing with her husband. When she indicated she was willing, Colin shared with his sister an alternate perspective through which to view her father and the way he showed affection. He helped her to see that perhaps their father had a different way of showing his love, like the way he provided for her and the family. He also suggested that other actions their father took, like staying up all night to assemble a dollhouse for her was another way he showed his affection.

Ultimately, he got his sister to see that she was taking their father's actions personally when they had nothing to do with her. When she was able to comprehend what her brother meant, he helped her to see the correlation between her father and her hubby. The light bulb moment happened when her brother pointed out that her marriage was not the first relationship she had where her mate did not show affection. He helped her to see the role her soul played in helping her to heal by attracting opportunity after opportunity for the childhood wound to be resolved. For the unworthiness that was controlling her to be replaced with her understanding that the affection scenarios did not define her worthiness.

Julie finally arrived at a place of gratitude towards her husband and his unwitting role in her healing. She dropped the anger and her behavior towards him changed. Almost like magic, his daughter returned to her own home and Julie and her husband entered into a new phase of their relationship. Mission accomplished from their souls' perspective, their marriage continued and was better than ever.

Radical forgiveness is essential to living your best life. Holding on to anger, pain, and resentment from unresolved experiences requires a tremendous amount of energy. Forgiveness allows the energy to be transmuted, infused with renewed vibrations for manifesting the goodness inside of you that is poised to pour forth as your best life.

You create space for manifesting. You create space for new ideas to flow to you. You're able to move in a lighter, more intentional way because you're no longer bogged down by the unforgiveness masquerading as heavy, dense obstacles. Radical forgiveness is not for the weak. It is for people who are ready to ditch the bags of victimhood and reclaim their power. It is for people who are willing to consider that unresolved hurts from past experiences, some from childhood, could be the underlying factor in unworthiness that attracts recurring adulthood issues.

The radical forgiveness approach is also a reminder that relationships come bearing gifts if we're willing to accept that the work to improve any relationship begins with you. To use the radical forgiveness approach, go to RadicalForgiveness.com, click on the "Free Resources" tab and download the Radical Forgiveness and the Radical Self-Forgiveness worksheets. Follow the instructions for completing the forms and repeat the process as often as necessary to heal. Also, it might be necessary to seek the support of a trained therapist to help you navigate traumatic events surrounding your forgiveness work.

# DEVOTION

By Maurice White / Philip Bailey
Performed by Earth, Wind and Fire

Through devotion
Blessed are the children
Praise the teacher
That brings true love to many
Your devotion
Opens all life's treasures, yeah
And deliverance
From the fruits of evil

So our mission
To bring a melody
Ringin' voices, woo hoo
Sing sweet harmony

For you here's a song
To make your day brighter
One that will last you long
Through troubled days
Giving your heart, ooh
The light to brighten
Oh, oh, oh, all of the dark
That falls in your way

You need devotion
Bless the children, whoa
Deliverance
From the fruits of evil

In everyone's life
There's a need to be happy
Let the sun shine
A smile your way
Open your heart
Feel a touch of devotion
Maybe this song
Will help uplift your day
Make a better way
You need devotion
You need devotion
Bless the children
Deliver from the fruits of evil

You need devotion
You need devotion
Bless the children
Why don't you bless the children
Deliver from the fruits of evil
You need devotion
You need devotion
Bless the children

# CHAPTER 6

# WORTHY AND GRATEFUL

Ultimately, forgiving every version of yourself, becoming aware that you're innately worthy and normalizing the presence of your authenticity will provide a degree of clarity that changes everything. The puzzle pieces fall into place, your life makes sense and feeling grateful takes on new meaning because regretting who you were and what you did or didn't do no longer makes sense.

Gratitude becomes a mainstay and leaks into all aspects of your life. It's the perfect time to become even more intentional about gratitude. The reconnection to your innate worth gets a boost when you make gratitude a part of the journey. When gratitude is a part of your day, your focus is on what's right instead of what's wrong and what you have, instead of what you don't have. Gratitude helps you see your life from a higher perspective and because spiritual law is always working, it attracts experiences that match gratitude's positive energy.

Now it's time to maximize the gratitude because maximizing gratitude keeps you in the energetic frequency of worthiness and makes living from it an easier, more fluid experience. Making gratitude a way of life conditions your mind to look for and expect the best and makes habits that emerge from unworthiness unacceptable. When gratitude is deliberate, complaining loses its luster. When gratitude is a priority, gossiping feels like the childish waste of energy it is. When you're intentional about gratitude, settling, shrinking and dimming your light feel disrespectful.

When you focus on gratitude, you are better able to take control of your thoughts. In my favorite book about gratitude, the bestselling, *Thank and Grow Rich*, author Pam Grout says embracing gratitude shuts off the critical voice in our minds. "When we don't stop daily to inventory all the gazillion things going right in our lives, the crazy voices in our heads try to make us their bitch."

Without gratitude as a regular component of your life, you have no control over those crazy voices, they control you. Gratitude has a powerful impact on how you see yourself, how you see others and how you see your world. With it, your glass is half-full, and not in a Pollyann-ish way. Gratitude improves your outlook on life and the way you move through your days just feels different.

Challenges and problems continue, but gratitude helps you see the bigger picture and you're more likely to pursue solutions instead of being bogged down with the problems. When you practice gratitude long enough, you continue transforming the content of your subconscious mind. The shifted content sparked by self-forgiveness expands and is joined by more powerful, affirming ideas that serve you, not stymie you.

Gratitude makes responding to life an easier choice. Gratitude and worthiness go hand in hand. Gratitude helps develop your compassion. Gratitude helps you walk away from situations that used to pull some other reaction from you. With gratitude as a staple, your core attitude shifts because it helps you to see that most of what used to aggravate you really ain't that serious. You're more likely to cut yourself and others some slack because gratitude makes it easier to stop sweating the small stuff.

Gratitude makes it possible for things that used to get on your last nerve to now be a source of amusement. Some of it might even crack you up. Understanding the power of your thoughts is an incentive for embracing gratitude because you cannot focus on gratitude and think negatively. Gratitude and positive thinking are travel buddies and both generate great energy, which attracts matching experiences and relationships.

Gratitude changes your life. Most people think unintentionally. Remember that humans think an average of 60,000 thoughts each day, of which 90 percent are repetitive and 80 percent are negative. The more you focus on gratitude, the fewer negative thoughts you think. And the fewer negative thoughts you think, the fewer negative experiences you have.

Gratitude has helped me navigate seeming disappointments. Gratitude develops a big picture mindset that sees beyond circumstances, like believing that when you don't get the job it's because there's something better. Gratitude doesn't stop challenging life experiences from happening, but it helps you to see them through different lenses. A grateful mentality expands your worth consciousness, and vice versa. Each fuels the other.

As your experience with gratitude continues, you will eventually evolve from being grateful for what happens in your life to being grateful *before* things happen. Gratitude works in concert with faith – which is absolutely essential to creating a life you love. When you get to that point, where you can feel grateful for something you want to manifest before you manifest it, you've graduated to the big leagues are it's game on!

As you take control of your thoughts, forgive past hurts, and make gratitude a more prominent part of your life, your energy will be transformed. As you eliminate negative thinking, embrace self-forgiveness and practice radical forgiveness, the amazing aspects of your personality that had been concealed beneath unworthiness, non-forgiveness and negativity have space to expand. When you begin meditating (which we'll talk about in the next chapter), discovering wonderful qualities and characteristics about yourself and zeroing in on gifts and talents with your name on them become a natural part of your journey.

As you encounter "new" parts of yourself and begin to acquaint yourself with the real you, gratitude reduces fear, worry and doubt. Getting to know the real you unleashes courage you didn't know you had because it's an organic part of your worthiness. The real you wants to be expressed. The energy of gratitude expedites the discovery, making it sweeter and more joyful because the energy of gratitude is positive, uplifting, feels good and is the engine that makes the law of attraction work favorably in your life.

The law of attraction is always working. It's the reason that thoughts held in mind produce after their kind. When you're aware of the power of your thoughts and you become intentional about thinking better thoughts, maximizing gratitude is like a positive thought turbo booster. As it relates to creating a life you love, the clarity surrounding what your best life looks like crystalizes, and obstacles that previously stood in your way are no longer an issue.

The combination of thinking better thoughts and maximizing gratitude is energizing, exhilarating actually because you begin to realize that you are more powerful than you realized. Discovering and creating a life you love is a joy in and of itself. The energy shift that comes from anticipating its manifestation is a beautiful experience made even more profound by gratitude, which plays a multifaceted role.

Another vital benefit of maximizing gratitude is the way focusing on what's right in your world helps you to stop comparing your life to someone else's. No one can live your best life, just as you cannot live someone else's. When you become more grateful for who you are, what you have, your experiences, your relationships, your life – wanting someone else's life does not make sense.

Discovering more about who you are is fascinating and fulfilling. It's a journey everyone should take but far too many actually do. People go their entire lives without discovering who they really are.

Authentic selves are born and buried without their owners' awareness.

Gratitude deepens your appreciation for you who are and what you bring to life's table. Gratitude helps you respect your journey and others' too. With gratitude as a mainstay, you set the stage to delve deeper into who you really are. The more grateful you are, the less space unworthiness takes up in your life. Gratitude is actually a pretty effective repellant that minimizes unworthiness while giving space for your worthiness to expand. Becoming intentional about gratitude is life-changing, especially if you're able to use it in EVERY situation, not just those that are clearly pleasant.

Sharpen your gratitude muscle by thinking about the last two experiences that stressed you out. Now that they're over, you can view them from a higher perspective, a vantage point that allows you to see how they blessed some aspect of your life. Even if it is simply that you made it through - there's a reason to be grateful. If you discovered something about yourself, that you're stronger, wiser, more resilient than you thought - those are reasons to be grateful.

Now take it a huge step forward by using a gratitude journal to help make being grateful a permanent part of your life. Purchase a lovely journal and at the end of each day, write down at least five things for which you are grateful. While the practice is designed for you to chronicle the day's gratitude each night, you move through your day mindful of the blessings you might not have noticed.

On those days where writing at least five gratitude moments is a challenge, flip back through older entries to be reminded of all the things you're grateful for. Although your days are full of experiences for which to be grateful, without an intention to maximize your gratitude, they could float right on past your awareness and you miss the opportunity to reap benefits from their beautiful energy.

# REJOICE

Steve Mac / Wayne Hector
Performed by The Emotions

If the things you do are not pleasing you
It's time to take another point of view
You take the things you've learned
All that you know are real
And what you feel is your first concern
Oh, then sacrifice and make it right

Rejoice in the things you know are right
You better rejoice
Make you feel real good inside

There may be times, oh, when you're in doubt
About the way
And just how to work it all out
You'll find the things you seek
Are within your reach
Your mind conceived it
Your heart will believe it
Now that you've sacrificed and you've
Paid the price
To make a better way in your life today rejoice
You can see the light, yes you can ah yeah

Rejoice ahh yeah, yeah
There may be times, oh, when you're in doubt
About the way
And just how to work it all out
You'll find the things you seek
Are within your reach
Your mind conceived it
Your heart will believe it
Now that you've sacrificed
And you've paid the price to
Make a better way in your life today

CHAPTER 7

# WORTHINESS IS SPIRITUAL

If you've grown up with a strong allegiance to a religion that was introduced to you in childhood, it might be difficult to consider any other way of thinking. Ideally, religion should enhance your life, especially since it means to "bind together," and its most predominant factor is meant to be love. Religion should be a beautiful experience.

Ultimately humanity's relationship with religion is what humanity determines it is, collectively and individually. Embraced and embodied as intended, religion is a sacred, expansive journey to experience the Divine, a deeply loving foundation for living. Religion is also man-made, however, and in many regards, man's interpretation and use of religion have often appeared to be anything but loving.

Facets of it are punitive, judgmental and include a significant amount of patriarchal beliefs designed to keep women "in their place." Some of it was used to justify slavery and the same colonized messaging has been preserved in many churches, some Black; infused with gospel music and a more soulful message.

Religion differs from spirituality in significant ways. Religion is an externally focused, collective experience with rules and regulations followers are expected to observe. Many religions were created as control mechanisms that inspire a fear of God and the belief that despite being made in God's image and likeness, humans are not worthy of God's blessings.

Spirituality is an individual experience with the Divine; an inwardly focused journey to discover the sacred within humanity. Because you're naturally spiritual, and the basis that constitutes your best life is within you, personalizing spirituality is essential for discovering and revealing the best version of yourself. As a spiritual being, you came here worthy but without a regular spiritual practice, you might not be aware of its power and that your worthiness can be used intentionally.

Deepening your spirituality does not require severing your connection to religion, but it does encourage examining the role it plays in becoming the real you. It encourages you to take a closer look at how it informs your thoughts about yourself and your world. It encourages you to question aspects you might not understand fully or that just don't feel right.

One of the disadvantages of religion has been its seeming mandate for unconditional, total acceptance; even though the staunchest religious believers pick and choose portions of religion that suit them while discarding aspects that don't. Swarms of people have defected from religion, some due to confusing experiences that made them feel persecuted and judged for being human.

If you have sworn off religion, that's commendable because it means, perhaps, you've thought critically about whether religion is right for you. There are millions of others who continue practicing a religion they no longer believe in or understand out of fear of disappointing others. For some of you, your rejection of religion might have also included a rejection of spirituality, assuming it's like religion. It's not.

Spirituality is as natural as your breath and effective for getting beyond the misconceptions religion conveys about your worthiness. Some spiritual movements, like New Thought, help decipher the non-literal meanings of religious terms that are used to control people with fear and threats of eternal punishment.

Religion tells you what to do, why you must do it and what happens if you don't. Spirituality shows you who you are, who you can become and opens you to the possibilities. There are things about yourself you can only discover by going within and spirituality is the vehicle to take you there.

As it relates to creating a life you love, personalizing spirituality ensures you are not leaving precious aspects of yourself undiscovered, critical since your best life is a reflection of your authentic self.

Spirituality is about YOUR journey to experience the divine. While reading about it and practicing spiritual ideas and deepening your understanding about it are all critical parts of the journey, it's not until you experience the divine for yourself that you really get a taste of what it means to be a spiritual being having a spiritual experience in human form. You will know when you've experienced God for yourself. You don't need a middle man to manage or label your experience. You are divinity. God doesn't exist separately from you.

Religion requires obedience rooted in duality, the belief that God is a man in the sky with the power to monitor, judge and ultimately punish people who fall short of God's mandates. My spiritual journey began as an attempt to understand and appreciate religion. I share it to show what it looks like to explore the traditional, seemingly mandated approach to religion, and why I eventually gave myself permission to release it and replace it with a different belief system that felt more aligned.

The seeking began in earnest while I was in college and searching for something to fill the void I felt inside. I knew my life was missing something and because I only knew about religion, I assumed what I was looking for could be found in the church, so I dug deeper there. My family did not grow up immersed in religion and for reasons I did not understand until much later, I am grateful for that fact.

My maternal grandfather was a dynamic Church of God in Christ preacher who retired from the ministry before I was born. Growing up, I can count on one hand the number of times my family and I attended church. My brothers, cousins and I took pictures in our Easter outfits every year. My most vivid Easter memory was when my older brother, Tony, and I sat outside Antioch Baptist Church in Brownsville (Miami) during the service, munching on the candy we bought with the money we were supposed to place in the offering basket.

When I was around seven or eight, my mother took me with her to Cohen AME (African Methodist Episcopal) in Miami's Overtown neighborhood one Sunday. Ma had been seriously ill and, now recovered, she stood in front of the church to share her testimony. The adults cheered her on, many standing, clapping and shouting, especially when she paused to gather herself. I'd never seen anything like it and watching her get emotional made me emotional too. She chuckled a little when she rejoined me on the pew; squeezing my hand and whispering in my ear, "I didn't mean to make you cry."

I have vague memories of my mother receiving a small red cloth in the mail from a man named Reverend Ike. I had no idea what the cloth was for but knew prayer was somehow involved. When I learned, many, many years later, that his powerful ministry helped people understand that God is not a man in the sky, but a divine power presence everywhere, I really wished my mother had had the opportunity to worship with him in person. Undoubtedly, the most religious person in our family was my Aunt Vira (pronounced Viry), my mother's sister, older by a couple of years. She and my mother were extremely close, and she visited our house often.

Each time she did, she was carrying her bible in one hand, a fashionable designer purse in the other. Aunt Vira used to be dressed to the nines, too. She always wore heels and either a pretty dress or a skirt with a matching top. Hair always on point and perfectly applied make-up matched the loving, jovial energy that always preceded her. I adored Aunt Vira.

When I was around eight or nine, Aunt Vira's youngest daughter, my cousin/best friend Charlotte, was the same age and my baby brother, Nealon, was around four. Concerned that we were not attending anybody's Sunday school and therefore not learning anything about Jesus and the Bible, Aunt Vira coaxed the three of us into a friendly competition with $20 going to the winner. She gave us a Bible and a few days to memorize its books. With the money as an incentive, we got busy studying. I won, Charlotte took second and Nealon got an honorary mention and five bucks just for trying.

A couple of years later, my mother's illness returned and took a turn for the worse. Ma died on November 8, 1974. I was 11-years old and at Aunt Vira's house when the telephone rang early the next morning. Lying in one twin bed while Charlotte slept in the other, I heard Aunt Vira outside the closed door when she broke the news to her teenage daughter, Tawanna. I jumped up, confused, crying, screaming but feeling like no sound was coming from me.

No one talked about her illness and I had no idea my mother was so sick. Ma knew she was dying of metastatic breast cancer so she had taken care of everything beforehand, including making arrangements with Aunt Vira to assume custody of Nealon and me. Apparently, my aunt agreed to do so before my mother died, but shortly after Ma transitioned, changed her mind based on some dynamics that I'm still not clear about.

Years later when I became an adult, a wife and a mother, I tried to consider what might have prompted Aunt Vira to renege; thought about the myriad responsibilities adults manage and without knowing for sure what transpired, I forgave her. My aunt died in the early 90s. Years before she transitioned, I lived with her briefly while in high school. I have fond memories, especially of the early mornings when I'd be running late, and we'd hop in her red Camaro to race down the city bus.

We never discussed her broken promise. I only share the story to help explain my early relationship with religion and the conflicting ideas my young mind began to develop about it because it was my first time seeing church folk say or do things I didn't understand. The next would be when my grandfather decided we should remember our mother as she was when she was alive, and Nealon and I were not allowed to view her body or attend the funeral. Granddaddy meant well but his decision was an unhealthy intrusion on our grieving process that prolonged it and left emotional wounds that lingered well into adulthood.

My baby brother and I ended up living with Aunt Maxine, Uncle Delton and their four children, Derrick, Mel, Sherri and Venice. We never attended church, which was fine with me. I recall Aunt Maxine once saying she wanted us to feel free to choose a religion that suited us when we became adults – a position I respect immensely.

I didn't entertain the idea of religion or church until I went away to Florida State University in 1981. Something was stirring in me and I sensed that being in church would sooth it, so I visited a few before joining St. Mary's Baptist Church near the FSU campus. Although I enjoyed the services, there was something I couldn't quite put my finger on that always left me feeling guilty, confused or aching for more.

I continued attending, but sporadically, eventually finding my way to a Church of God in Christ near my apartment. I was captivated by the loud, enthusiastic music, the amazing choir and the rousing sermons. That the congregation got "happy" with regularity was amusing, but frustrating because this happiness-inducing "Holy Ghost" took hold of my fellow college coeds and the senior citizens - everybody except me. I remember thinking there was something wrong with me or there had to be something I wasn't doing. I wanted to experience what everyone else was experiencing, so I clapped louder, stood and swayed. I closed my eyes like the older women and waited for the Holy Ghost to show up.

Meanwhile, I was also struggling to understand heaven and hell, sin, the Bible and living righteously. I was in church every week. One Sunday, certain this was my lucky day, I stood up, clapped, sang along and although overcome with emotion, I could tell it wasn't the Holy Ghost. Other people were falling out, speaking in tongues, sweating and being surrounded by ushers to catch them when they collapsed.

This Holy Ghost seemed to be an important, necessary part of the religious experience. So how come it was skipping over me? Maybe I needed to join the church, I reasoned, so I made my way to the front when the pastor extended the invitation. As I stood there, not a partier, hardly a drinker, but sexually active with my longtime boyfriend, something inside of me said joining the church was not the answer, so I quickly got an usher's attention and whispered to her, "I'm not ready," then walked out in the middle of the service and went home.

That was the last time I attended church in Tallahassee before returning to Miami in 1985. Graduation and marriage followed, and so did the inner stirring. Ex-hubby was nervous whenever we went to church because I would inevitably drag him with me down front to either receive prayer or join. We ended up becoming members at New Way Baptist church in Miami Gardens and it wasn't long before my big, tormenting questions started. Did heaven and hell really exist? What's up with sin, repenting and being saved? Where, exactly, was God and how was it possible for Him to not only hear millions of prayers, but answer them, too?

Still not a big partier, a social drinker and now married, I didn't understand why I felt guilty following each sermon; and the confusion didn't let up either. I couldn't wrap my brain around the idea that by simply accepting Jesus as my personal Lord and Savior, I was "saved." If that's all there is to it and it's available to everyone, I reasoned that murderers and other people who intentionally hurt others could, by simply uttering a few words, be spared the condemnation that otherwise guaranteed them a place in hell.

With that formula, people could "sin" all their lives but just before dying, accept Jesus and be guaranteed safe passage to heaven. And speaking of heaven and hell, did God determine who got sent to burn based on one horrendous deed or could they commit that horrendous deed then perform dozens of good ones and go to heaven? What if the person had a violent street reputation, but while at home with his toddler son, was a doting father who taught him the alphabet and sign language?

That was my big brother, Skip, whom I absolutely adored. When I imagined him, an ex-con with a dangerous streak but also an awesome daddy to my nephew burning in hell based on the awful stuff he'd done, I needed to know whether his wonderful qualities were also a part of the equation. Did God weigh all that stuff? And what if Skip never got around to accepting Jesus? That was enough for me.

Skip was murdered on July 11, 1989 and I decided soon after his funeral that because hell didn't make sense, I would no longer concern myself with it. And when I heard, years later, the Pope himself said publicly that heaven and hell are not places, but states of mind, I was done.

(Fast forward to 2023: I posted social media messages about why I ditched the whole heaven and hell belief system and well-meaning religious people reached out to help save my soul. I've been on an extremely gratifying, life-changing spiritual journey for decades and lovingly informed them that while I appreciate their concern, I am completely thrilled with my metaphysical understanding and beliefs regarding where spiritual beings go when they transition.)

In the late 80s, after trying in vain to feel more at ease at New Way by becoming involved in volunteering and activities, I stopped going altogether. At some point after giving up on church, I was flipping through a magazine or newsletter and saw a prayer that resonated with me so deeply I cut it out and stuck it in my pocket. I read it a few more times and eventually misplaced it.

By this time, I'd discovered a book called *You Can Heal Your Life* by Louise Hay that I devoured. Very spiritual, it focuses on the power of forgiveness, healing, self-approval and self-love. I was blown away that Louise Hay had healed herself of cancer by using the power of her thoughts, forgiveness, spiritual work and nutrition.

Other spiritual books began to line my shelves and Susan Taylor's "In the Spirit" column was also feeding my soul. It was a major reason I looked forward to Essence magazine each month. It was always the first thing I read because her message centered on self-care, loving yourself and each other, authenticity, discovering your purpose, giving back – meaningful topics that resonated with my core.

In 1994, I was working as the manager of the Florida Foster Care Review Project. One day my boss, Julia Cope, and I were in my office chatting when the conversation turned to why we'd stopped attending church. Although she's Caucasian and I'm African-American, we'd both had similar experiences and many of the same unanswered questions. Julia got excited when she recalled a recent discussion with a dear friend who told her about a different kind of church with a pastor who "was full of himself," but also deeply spiritual and skilled at helping "seekers" make sense of religion.

"Look, if you stand right here, you can see it," Julia said from behind me as she literally turned my head to see the tall white building with the word UNITY atop a few miles southeast of our office. Intrigued, I stopped by during my lunch break. I had no idea whether the church was open, but my intuition said to find its exact location so I'd know how to get there on Sunday. The church was closed, but not the bookstore.

As soon as I entered, the energy, the peacefulness, the subtle smell of incense felt welcoming and familiar. The cashier looked up from the glass display and smiled. "Let me know if you need any help." I was mesmerized. The shelves were lined with books, many of which I had at home, and the eclectic jewelry displayed throughout the shop were pieces I could definitely see myself rocking. Spirited artwork, candles and other earthy merchandise made time stand still in this surreal space, then one book caught my eye.

Propped on the shelf with its full title visible, not shelved like the other books was *You Can Heal Your Life*. By now, I was covered in goosebumps, tearfully trying to contain my emotions. A few deep breaths helped me regroup, and after browsing a little more, I bought incense and a box of You Can Heal Your Life inspirational cards before returning to my office.

I could hardly wait the few days before Sunday arrived. Walking into the foyer of Unity on the Bay felt like Deja vu. There on the wall was a big, beautiful tapestry with a prayer stitched on it. I knew immediately it was the prayer, the one I'd cut out of the magazine.

*The light of God surrounds us.*
*The love of God enfolds us.*
*The power of God protects us.*
*The presence of God watches over us.*
*Wherever we are, God is.*
*And all is well.*

Confirmation! I was home. Not only was this very soothing prayer (The Prayer of Protection) on the wall, we also recited it at the end of the sermon. That was the first time my daughters Alexandra (8), Stephanie, (18 months) and I visited the church I would attend for over 20 years. Everything about it felt right, especially the guided meditation, preceded by a beautiful song that deepened my interest in understanding the power of my thoughts.

*Our thoughts are prayers,*
*And we are always praying,*
*Our thoughts are prayers,*
*Listen to what you're saying,*
*Seek a higher consciousness,*
*A state of peacefulness,*
*And know that God is always there.*
*And every thought becomes a prayer.*

Rev. James Trapp, the "full of himself" pastor of this beautifully diverse congregation was full of grace, wisdom, gentle humor and spiritual brilliance that grew the congregation from a few hundred when he was appointed as its senior minister in the early-90s, to more than a thousand in no time. I'd finally found a church with a message that made sense to me at one of the oldest New Thought ministries in existence. For once, I felt wonderful in church and like I was floating when I left. I felt empowered and relieved to know God was not the bearded old man in the sky, but an ever- present, all loving power, always flowing, always blessing, always good.

I gained a new understanding and deep appreciation for Jesus, our Way Shower who encouraged us to do everything He did and more. Worshiping Jesus as God used to confuse me, so to learn that Christ wasn't his last name, but the state of divinity within Jesus that He ascended to and fully embodied; and that it also exists within us SET ME FREE. Learning that Jesus was passionately interested in teaching us to love radically and unconditionally SET ME FREE.

New Thought spirituality helped me to understand my divinity and answered so many of the questions religion could not answer for me. It introduced me to my power, helped me release some of the limiting beliefs I had about myself and inspired me to get to know the real Michelle.

I share my journey to these beautiful spiritual teachings to encourage you to examine your own journey to whatever religious or spiritual beliefs you currently hold. Taking a look at what you believe and how you've arrived at those beliefs really helps you understand yourself at deeper levels. Exploring how you were introduced to your religious or spiritual beliefs is an eye-opener if you did not choose the religion you practice.

Judging the introduction isn't necessary, but understanding it is. Check in with your intuition for guidance on how to proceed. If you're holding back because you're afraid to disappoint others, you never know, they may have some of the very same questions. Asking questions of anything you don't fully understand is fundamental to learning and growing. Personal development simply cannot happen without it.

Consider this: There is religious scripture that literally encourages harm to women. Thankfully, Bible readers have become more selective over the years and are willing to ignore or reinterpret verses that call for non-virgins to be stoned, for example.

As you contemplate your journey to reconnecting to your innate worthiness, look at the impact your religion has on you and how you live your life. Religious beliefs that limit your full expression as a spiritual being should be questioned. Religious beliefs that say you're unworthy of goodness, and unworthy of God's blessings, unworthy period, should be analyzed. Religious beliefs that threaten to punish you for expressing all aspects of you – including your sexuality – should be re-examined.

Living the life you're meant to live is impossible without giving major thought to beliefs you might have been introduced to as a child. Now that you're an adult, do they serve you or stifle you? If you can understand that your best life is an inside-out job then you can embrace just how important your spiritual life is. There is no way to get to know the real you without spending time in the silence and meditating. Don't be scared. You don't have to sit cross legged for hours and clear your mind to meditate. It's about getting still, breathing deeply, relaxing your body and paying attention to your thoughts.

Delving regularly into the silence reveals qualities, characteristics, gifts, talents, desires, wisdom, faith, imagination and more – all ingredients for creating a life you love which flows from your innate worth. It also helps you make sense of the difficulties in your life, like childhood trauma and experiences that made you feel unworthy.

Spending time alone in the silence is a beautiful practice, but it's also essential for discovering who you really are. It's what life's journey is really all about because everything you're meant to do flows from the truth of who you are - your authentic self - inside of you.

Silent solitude is also a time to explore new ideas about you, your life, your understanding of life's dynamics and the unlimited possibilities. It is exhilarating to encounter your own thoughts and to consider new ways of thinking that align with the full expression of your authenticity.

Following someone else's belief system is quite common. Millions of people belong to religions they did not choose for themselves. And many practice the requirements for their religion without questioning or fully realizing the impact on their life.

If you're afraid to question aspects of a religion because you're afraid of aspects of the religion, it's important for you to explore why. Are the religious beliefs you accepted as a child still valid now that you're an adult? Have you changed your perception of the beliefs or are you still embracing childish notions that don't make logical sense?

Anglican priest Richard Rohr, author of *The Universal Christ,* said many people practice "Kindergarten Christianity," a myopic, judgmental belief system with rules and regulations that are limiting and absent the unconditional love Jesus promoted. They grew up but their religious beliefs didn't.

What's your concept of God? Your answer to that question reveals a great deal about your perception of life and what you believe you deserve to experience. Your concept of God colors your beliefs about your worth and whether you even believe you are allowed to pursue some of the dreams you will discover. If you believe in a judgmental, punitive god, you might unknowingly foster underlying fear that blocks your discovery of your true self.

Believing a god is watching your every move and judging whether your actions are good or bad could stifle your efforts because you're treating this Supreme Power as though it were Santa Claus. If you believe in a god that has predetermined what your life will be, you might find it difficult to believe you have the power to manifest a life of your choosing. If you believe God is a man in the sky, you've bought into the idea of separation; that you and God are not One.

In addition to personifying God by assigning human tendencies like judgment, punishment, anger and jealousy to

Omniscience, if you believe in the devil or some satanic creature, you relinquish your power. Like other biblical content, scriptural reference to this entity is allegorical and not meant to be taken literally. Are you willing to consider a different perception that serves your growth and development instead of threatening arbitrary harm?

The metaphysical meaning of the "devil" is "error thinking." Its presence throughout the bible refers to the way humanity's negative, self-destructive thoughts harm its ability to live in alignment with God. Similarly, beliefs about heaven and hell could have an adverse impact on your motivation to manifest your best life, here and now.

Metaphysically, heaven and hell are not destinations you arrive at when you die but are instead states of consciousness. You create hell in your experiences by thinking negatively, refusing to forgive, and indulging in non-grateful behavior, among other limited, self-destructive thinking. Living under the spell of unworthiness could feel like living in hell because of the stressful experiences unworthiness attracts.

What you manifest when you believe you're unworthy reinforces your beliefs that you don't deserve better. Going to a job you hate, tolerating unhealthy, toxic relationships, struggling with your health and your finances and being preoccupied with other people's opinions are all "hellish" experiences that have no parts of a life you love.

When you're aligned with the truth of who you are and creating a life you love, you are experiencing heaven. When you have loving exchanges with others, you're experiencing heaven. When you experience the freedom forgiveness provides, you're experiencing heaven.

Religious beliefs that promote suffering now for a payoff after you die could make you feel guilty for having pleasurable experiences. All the more reason to examine your concept of God and whether it serves your life. Are you afraid of going to hell for enjoying certain natural aspects of living, like sex or having a glass of wine? Does your religion have you looking outside of yourself for something or someone to "save" you, and if so, what are you being saved from?

I pose these questions to encourage you to research your religion to understand its true meaning, gain deeper clarity regarding the context for scripture, learn who wrote biblical stories and why. Back in the day, religious leaders counted on people following them blindly, without questioning anything. That's no longer the case. If you're a part of a church with a minister that discourages questions, question that.

While I firmly believe spirituality, not religion, is instrumental to you living the life you're meant to live, it is important that you settle on what's right for YOU. If that means deepening your allegiance to your religion, do that. But do it with a spirit of customizing your beliefs to serve YOUR highest good.

It takes courage to personalize spirituality. It takes courage to examine commonly held beliefs and to determine whether they are for you or not. If they're not, it takes courage to release them and even more courage to replace them with what does work for you.

Personalizing spirituality is the most liberating act you can take because it undergirds everything you do. It sets you free, but you must be brave enough to allow Spirit to guide you to something that is already a part of you and is waiting for you to discover it. Personalizing spirituality provides a beautiful bridge to your innate worth, which has even more room to flourish when the space it exists in is free.

## Superpower Your Spirituality

Explore meditation. It's not complicated. Close your eyes. Take a deep breath, slowly inhaling and slowly exhaling. Do that for five minutes, playing attention to your breath. As thoughts come into your mind, don't fight them. Just let them float by, like clouds in the sky. That's meditation, which actually means to "pay attention to."

There's no right or wrong way. You're simply giving yourself the gift of relaxing in silent solitude with your thoughts and your breath. If you're new to meditation, you might want to start with a few short guided meditations on YouTube. You can also make meditation a practical experience.

If you're working toward a goal, there is very likely a guided meditation specifically focused on helping you achieve it. Set a daily morning schedule to meditate before you start your day. Before you check emails, social media or the news, give yourself the gift of silencing your mind and exposing it to tranquil, inspirational content that can elevate your consciousness.

Listening to a short guided meditation at night before you go to sleep gives your subconscious mind positive content to work with while you slumber. (DO NOT watch the news or anything negative before going to bed.)

*You can download my free Worthy Meditation at www.michellehollinger.com.*

# IN THE STONE

## By Allee Willis / Maurice White / David W. Foster
### Performed by Earth, Wind and Fire

I found that love provides the key
Unlocks the heart and souls of you and me
Love will learn to sing your song, yeah
Oh yeah, love is written in the stone

Every man I meet walking time
Free to wander past his conscious mind
Love will come and take you home, yeah
Yeah, love ah written in the stone

Do you believe, my friend in what you claim?
People of the world all doubt the same
Bringing questions of their own, yeah
Truth is, truth is written in the stone

In the stone (In the stone, you'll find the meaning)
(You're not standing tall)
In the stone (In the stone, the light is shining)
(Ever touching all)

Life experience a passing day
Time will witness what the old folks say
Getting stronger every day
Strength is, (strength... is written in the stone)

Deep inside your heart for you to keep
Lies a spark of light that never sleeps
The greatest love you ever known
Love is, love is written in the stone

In the stone (In the stone, you'll find the meaning)
(You're not standing tall)
It's in the stone (In the stone, the light is shining)
(Ever touching all)

Never, never, my darling
Never you'll be alone
Never, never, my darling
Never you'll be alone
Ever, forever, my darling
True love is written in the stone

Never, never my darling
Never you'll be alone
Ever, forever, my darling
True love is written in the stone
Never, never my darling
Never you'll be alone
Ever, forever, my darling
True love is written in the stone
Never
Ever
Written in the stone
Never
Written in the stone
Never

# CHAPTER 8

# NO WORTHINESS, NO PEACE
# KNOW WORTHINESS, KNOW PEACE

The life you're meant to live includes every part of you. It's not a fragmented experience where things are going well on the job, but your home life and health are in shambles. Or you take fabulous trips with your girls, but you come home to a toxic relationship. One of the loveliest results of taking control of your thinking, prioritizing forgiveness, maximizing gratitude and personalizing spirituality is the peace that becomes a permanent part of you.

And as Jon Kabat Zinn says in his book of the same title, "wherever you go, there you are." When you level up your consciousness, you awaken the connection to your worthiness, which sets you up for success, health, wealth, harmonious relationships, and allows your best life to unfold beautifully, from the inside-out. The peacefulness that already exists inside of you flows from you wherever you are – at work, at home, on a date, on vacation, in traffic.

Peace exists within you and is an indication of harmony and congruence. It is far more likely to exist when your thoughts, words and actions match up, and that alignment is an outcome of authenticity. Being someone you're not can never align with peace.

The most assured approach to loving your life is to create it from the inside out. Every experience you have begins with your thoughts, so it should go without saying that choosing better thoughts reduces stress. Forgiving yourself and others for stuff that had you stuck eliminates drama, and gratitude makes you feel so good you'll wonder what took you so long to make it a priority in your life. Personalizing spirituality is a gift that keeps on giving. The deeper you go, the deeper you'll want to go.

Together they transform your mindset and allow peace to flow from you in an increasingly effortless way. Eventually, you won't have to think about being peaceful, you'll simply be peaceful.

Aligning with your peace consciousness does not mean your life becomes perfect. Neither does it mean your challenges and trials disappear. It means that whatever happens, your response to it comes from a space of tranquility and calm assurance. It means you remain in control of your demeanor and that the first and most natural response comes from the peace that has expanded within you.

Peace allows you to respond instead of react. There's a big difference. Responding is a more thoughtful, centered approach. Reacting is knee-jerk and rooted in judgement and fear. The way you interact with everyone changes when you live from peace consciousness. Situations that used to aggravate you no longer have the same impact. On the rare occasion where your response is less than peaceful, returning to your peace takes less and less time. Operating from peace consciousness is a sweet part of manifesting your best life.

Peace consciousness dissolves worry. It feels good. It's not a Polly Anna existence that pretends problems don't exist. You just choose to see what's beneficial in a problematic situation. Instead of marinating in trouble, your mentality is about finding solutions.

When you become intentional about what you think, you're empowered to choose thoughts that contribute to your peace consciousness. You become more selective about the conversations you have and the people you spend time with. You are no longer interested in certain experiences because they simply do not align with your peacefulness.

Respecting others' points of view and choosing not to debate that point of view becomes easier and easier to embrace and you eventually master the art of minding your own business; one of the most peaceful, energy conserving practices you can adopt. It's perfectly okay for you to choose not to participate in stressful family discussions. You are allowed to refrain from responding to someone clearly operating from stress.

Living from your peace consciousness makes identifying what nurtures it easier. If something doesn't feel peaceful, it's not. Maximizing gratitude fuels peace consciousness since its focus is on goodness. The very nature of choosing to see goodness and positivity as much as you can activates and maintains your peace consciousness.

Continual maximization of gratitude, making it a regular part of your life, expands your peace consciousness. Something seemingly magical happens when your focus is primarily on what's right in your life. When you're not preoccupied with negativity you develop a drama repellant that helps you steer clear of foolishness. And when you're not constantly rehashing what's not working well, peace has space to flow freely and it becomes a wonderful habit.

Each idea contributes to your peace consciousness, however, prioritizing forgiveness plays the biggest role because of the baggage it allows you to eliminate. The energy necessary for holding on to resentment, anger, pain and grudges is dense and takes up valuable space. When you forgive, the dense energy that used to keep your past alive is transmuted into lighter, more sacred energy that organically fuses with and expands your peace consciousness.

When you do the work to heal wounds that kept you stuck, you free yourself to experience the innate peace that's been smothered by pain. Peace consciousness provides a soothing atmosphere from which your best life emerges. The calm, clarifying energy flowing from your peace consciousness makes it easier to say yes to what aligns with it and no to anything that doesn't. Not only that. Peace consciousness exudes a quiet confidence that allows you to be you unapologetically.

Your expanded peace consciousness attracts others operating from a similar space. Your circle changes. People who are not interested in a peaceful existence start to distance themselves from you and those who appreciate your aura move closer. The saying "what you do speaks so loudly I can't hear what you're saying," is very fitting, especially here.

Living from your peace consciousness is a lifestyle, a choice to indulge the inner realm where peace that passes all understanding awaits your attention. People pick up on your peace consciousness, not because you announce it, but because the way you move through life oozes peace and many people want some of that. Also, once living from peace consciousness becomes a habit, your ability to notice when an atmosphere isn't peaceful is heightened even if on the surface things appear calm. You notice the energy and when it's not peaceful, you know.

Years ago, whenever I was at a relative's home and the conversation shifted to gossip or complaints, without even thinking, I quietly left the room. Sometimes I might not have immediately realized that the discussion changed. What I'd notice was a shift in the energy. Since it wasn't in alignment with my peace, I did something about it. But not by requesting that others change their behavior. I'm responsible for my peace consciousness, so going into another room and reading a book, listening to music, watching something on television or joining a different conversation helped protect it.

I never announced my decision to remove myself from certain environments, never lectured others, or criticized their behavior, however, others noticed and years later, I was pleasantly surprised when a friend advised others that "when the gossip starts, Michelle's leaving." When you live from peace consciousness, its energy is evident and people not only notice it, they respect it.

Expanding your peace consciousness also has a beautiful impact on your health. All illness is impacted by stress in your body. Stress produces cortisol and when present in the body for extended periods, it creates sickness. As a spiritual being having a human experience, health is your birthright. Your baseline is meant to be health and your peace consciousness helps solidify it.

All of the work to activate your innate worth and engage your authenticity has ripple effects that elevate every aspect of your life. Your wealth, your health, your relationship with yourself and others, your professional life, your personal life - every aspect gets a boost.

# I CHOOSE

Mark Christopher Batson / India Arie / Andrew Luis Castro
Performed by India.Arie

Because you never know where life is gonna take you
and you can't change where you've been.
But today, I have the opportunity to choose.

Here am I now looking at 30 and I got so much to say.
I gotta get this off of my chest, I gotta let it go today.
I was always too concerned about what everybody would
think.
But I can't live for everybody, I gotta live my life for me.
(Yeah)

I pitched a fork in the road of my life and ain't nothing gonna
happen unless I decide.
to be the best that I can be.

(I choose) to be authentic in everything I do.
My past don't dictate who I am. I choose. (Yeah)

I done been through some painful things I thought that I
would never make it through.
Filled up with shame from the top of my head to the soles of
my shoes.
I put myself in so many chaotic circumstances, but by the
grace of God I've been given so many second chances.

But today I decided to let it all go. I'm dropping these bags,
I'm making room for my joy.
to be the best that I can be.

(I choose) to be authentic in everything I do.
My past don't dictate who I am. I choose.
Because you never know where life is gonna take you and
you can't change where you've been.
But today, I have the opportunity to choose. (Hey ey)

I used to have guilt about why things happen they way they
did cuz life is gone do what it do.
And everyday, I have the opportunity to choose.

From this day forward I'm going to be exactly who I am.
I don't need to change the way that I live just to get a man.
(NO!)
I even had a talk with my mama and I told her the day I'm
grown,
"from this day forward, every decision I make will be my
own." And hey!
to be the best that I can be.

(I choose) to be courageous in everything I do.
My past don't dictate who I am. I choose.
to be the best that I can be.
(I choose) to be authentic in everything I do.

My past don't dictate who I am. I choose.

Because you never know where life is gonna take you and you can't change where you've been.
But today, I have the opportunity to choose. (Hey ey)
I used to have guilt about why things happen they way they did cuz life is gone do what it do.
And everyday, I have the opportunity to choose.

# CHAPTER 9

# WORTHY TO BE WEALTHY

Prosperity is your birthright. Lack is learned. You were not born to struggle. You're meant to thrive and have more than enough. If these statements make you feel anything other than, "damn right!" - there's a mindset shift around money you deserve to experience.

Prosperity actually means "spiritual wellbeing" and you are meant to live prosperously in your finances, your health, your relationships, your career, and throughout your entire existence. Some have a fragmented understanding about prosperity, believing that having more than enough money would make struggling through other experiences - like health issues or relationship problems or career woes - easier.

Prosperity is an inside-out harmonious experience that flows beautifully into and defines every aspect of your life, making struggling as a way of life extremely unlikely. Prosperity is about money but so much more. Embodying it in every aspect of your being is essential to loving your life.

Being stressed out because you don't have enough money and not being able to afford the things that bring you joy is an unfortunate narrative that far too many people have been taught. It's a way of life that many believe is normal but the truth is prosperity is your birthright.

Money and worthiness are intertwined, unfortunately. Many believe if you have money you're worthy and if you don't, you're not. Admittedly, my pervasive money troubles as an adult were steeped in deep seated unworthiness that originated in my childhood. Living through traumatic experiences while also not having enough money convinces you subconsciously that not only are you not enough, but that you also do not deserve to have enough. Knowing you're worthy helps heal that mindset.

Shifting to wealth requires a shift in mindset. A common sentiment that normalizes being poor "because we were happy" romanticizes scarcity consciousness, creating an underlying thread of guilt for anyone wanting something better. You cannot prosper from guilt. You cannot manifest beyond an internal set-point tied to not upsetting people in your family who have not healed their poverty mindset because they don't know how. And if their inability to rise above their circumstances frustrates them in ways they might not be able to express, your efforts to prosper can feel like a personal attack.

Your worthiness empowers you to dissolve inner turmoil surrounding prosperity. It strengthens your discernment and compassion and frees you to understand others' plight without feeling obligated to join them. It liberates your consciousness to release lack, limitation and scarcity so that your true God-given prosperity has room to expand.

For many Black people, it's important to also examine the country's relentless agenda to strip their ancestors of financial abundance and how its blatant monetary discrimination contributed to many Black people's impoverished survival mindset. Generational poverty is a stubborn and deeply entrenched dysfunction that is maintained by rigid belief systems with unworthiness as a factor.

The increasing focus on acquiring generational wealth represents a beautiful mindset shift regarding money and prosperity. Thankfully, it acknowledges the origin of generational poverty and includes efforts to transform the thought process from survival-based to thriving-focused. Making generational worthiness a prevailing pattern equips families to prosper.

## About Survival Skills

Your worthiness helps you dislodge and eliminate the stubborn lack and limitation mindsets resulting from childhood money beliefs. For example, many of us learned valuable survival skills from not having enough, like "how to make grits grocery," and how to skillfully "rob Peter to pay Paul." But healing a poverty mentality helps differentiate between having those skills and having to use them. You know how to perform CPR, but you're not hoping for an emergency where it's necessary.

Embracing and celebrating survival skills tells your subconscious mind to create circumstances to use them. Your worthiness, on the other hand, helps you feel grateful for the times you needed them, while also inspiring you to replace them with softer, healthier, more prosperity-aligned habits.

Importantly, if you are still using the survival skills you learned while growing up poor, that's proof that an internalized, impoverished, fear-based belief system is still running your life. Your worthiness can fix that. Since the majority of your thoughts about money were planted during your childhood, if you struggle with money now, you owe it to yourself to examine your beliefs about it and determine where they came from.

My family was poor. After my parents divorced, my single mother worked hard to provide for us, but we struggled. We received food stamps and there were things we couldn't do because we didn't have the money to do them. When you adjust to doing without, you unwittingly train your mind and consciousness to expect to do without - and expectations are powerful!

Unexamined, unhealed, not knowing what you don't know allows childhood expectations to become lodged in your belief system and morph into your adult way of thinking.

## You Experience What You Expect

Expecting to always have money problems is revealed in your perception about daily money experiences that feel normal. Expectations create a way of thinking and behaving that become personality traits that you do not question. How often do you complain about how much things cost? Are you preoccupied with finding cheaper products and services? Do you look for ways to get something for nothing?

Being frugal is one thing. If the reason behind the frugality is a scarcity mindset and fear of not having enough, it keeps scarcity and not having enough on your radar and in your experiences.

In his classic masterpiece on prosperity, *Spiritual Economics*, Eric Butterworth said, "The starting point in realizing prosperity is to accept responsibility for your own thoughts, thus taking charge of your life…Refuse to indulge in casual conversation about the bad economy, the high cost of living, or about anything you really do not want to say "yes" to.

Eliminate such thoughts as "I can't," "I'm afraid," and "There is not enough" from your consciousness." Contrary to popular belief, prosperity and poverty are both states of mind.

How you think about money determines your relationship with it and your relationship with money informs how it shows up in your life.

If you do things you don't want to do for money – like going to a job you hate because it pays the bills and affords you a certain lifestyle - you owe it to yourself to explore your relationship with money and how worthiness factors into it. Similarly, if there are things you're unable to do because you don't have enough – like passing up on opportunities, denying yourself that trip, living someplace that doesn't really align with your true desires, automatically shopping in certain stores or other circumstances you have probably grown so accustomed to, assessing your relationship with the green stuff could be helpful.

You might believe the key to transforming your financial status means focusing on ways to increase your income, learning about investments and perhaps how to save your money. Those are great ideas and tools for growing your money, but that's not where we focus to align with and expand our prosperity consciousness. If you do all those things without changing your mindset about money, the underlying stress about not having enough will continue to fester.

Bottom line is money is energy and it responds to our thoughts and feelings about it. Thoughts steeped in scarcity repel money and unless we shift our thoughts about it we remain in a cycle of struggle with perhaps occasional financial relief. Everything about creating a life you love, including transforming your relationship with money, is an inside-out process that begins with your thoughts and with accepting you're a spiritual being having a human experience.

As a spiritual being you operate under spiritual law, whether you're aware of it or not. Spiritual law, like gravity, doesn't need our awareness to function. It is in motion at all times and our thoughts interact with it and manifest the predominant pattern of our thinking. We don't get what we want, we get what we are. And if our predominant thoughts are centered in lack and limitation, that's what we experience.

People who have lots of money but are afraid they'll lose it or who work incessantly to keep and increase what they have at the expense of other aspects of their lives are operating from a scarcity mentality, despite their riches. They're beholden to the money because they don't understand the true power necessary for its manifestation.

Unworthiness makes it impossible to feel prosperous and will result in you repelling money without understanding why. You can do all the "right" things as far as working hard, saving money and trying to spend it wisely; but because you can never have more than you feel worthy of having, there will always be an impenetrable ceiling that slides into place. People know money is necessary for living well, but feel guilty about wanting it.

It's why some people can suddenly come into large amounts of money but lose it all. If their money mindset is steeped in unworthiness, their physical reality will adjust to the stronger underlying beliefs. There's no amount of work you can do externally to alleviate a sense of unworthiness. Going within and doing the work to reconnect to your innate worth is the only remedy.

Reconnecting to your worthiness, cultivating and expanding it makes prosperity possible because feeling worthy shifts your beliefs about what you deserve to receive. You can have an outward appearance of a prosperous life but suffer privately because despite the increase in your income, you're still thinking the same limited money thoughts and having the same limited money experiences - but on a larger scale.

Iyanla Vanzant is an excellent example of someone who earned lots of money but because she still had the poverty mentality she learned as a little girl, her experiences with money as a successful adult remained anchored in lack, limitation and fear. The author, spiritual leader and former TV host explained that because she was raised on welfare and her family always ran out of money and food stamps before month's end, even as a millionaire she believed she had to use all of her money before she received more. Her poverty mentality resulted in her using her millions the same way her family used their public assistance and food stamps.

When she did her mental and spiritual work and healed her poverty-based ideas about money, Iyanla created a clean slate for herself and rebuilt her life. Thankfully, she's completely transparent about her journey from a poverty to prosperity mentality so that others can learn from her experience.

Thoughts held in mind produce after their kind in every single area of your life – including your finances. Living a life you love requires complete alignment with and expansion of your prosperity consciousness. Aligning with your prosperity consciousness requires awareness of its importance in creating and maintaining financial freedom.

I speak from experience because aligning with and expanding my prosperity consciousness and healing my relationship with money has been a major focus of my journey. Understanding that so much of my financial belief system stems from what I learned and observed as a child has helped me to unravel my limiting beliefs about money. Shifting from a sense of unworthiness to embracing my innate worth and creating space for my authentic self to BE had a major impact on my relationship with money.

When you're operating under the spell of unworthiness, even if you have an intellectual understanding of how to earn lots of money, the underlying belief that you don't deserve it will keep you struggling to manifest and maintain it. The healthier my relationship with money, the easier it is for me to manifest it.

Pointing the finger at the economy, your boss, your bills or the devil instead of taking responsibility for your prosperity will keep you delving in scarcity. Your money woes don't just happen to you. There's nothing coincidental about struggling from paycheck to paycheck. Your thoughts about money and your thoughts about yourself are at the root of all your financial concerns. Every single one.

Religious beliefs of a judgmental god in the sky, the mistaken belief of poverty as a virtue as well as the misleading scriptural reference to money being the root of all evil creates conflicting mindsets in many people. The scripture actually says the *love* of money is the root of evil, referring to an obsession with money above all else.

Peeling back the layers of your beliefs about money, prosperity and poverty is necessary for creating a life you love. Struggling financially and living fully don't coexist. Ultimately, you must get clear that your thoughts and beliefs about money determine your relationship with it. Negative ideas about money must be tossed away – so it's necessary to examine their origin and use a mature perspective to poke holes in unwarranted beliefs that might have been lurking beneath the surface, but informing the way you live, nonetheless.

Money is sacred. Money is good. Money really is God in action. Coming to terms with these ideas might take some work, but the work is worth it. Ultimately, your worth consciousness determines your prosperity consciousness. Doing the work to awaken your worthiness empowers you to attract the financial abundance you deserve.

Discovering and relishing the awesomeness that you are makes you magnetic to experiences that align with it. Expanding your worth consciousness strengthens your ability to manifest more - from the inside out.

## Superpower Your Prosperity

Affirming that you are prosperous sends the message to your subconscious mind to accept expansive, abundant beliefs. Affirming I AM PROSPEROUS gets the prosperity ball rolling. And because spiritual law either brings you what you affirm or what's standing in the way of it, you might encounter push back from the scarcity crowd taking up space in your subconscious mind.

That's cool. Now you know what to work on. See, it's impossible to heal what's concealed. When you affirm I AM PROSPEROUS, become mindful of any opposing thoughts, not to study and give energy, but to become aware of so that when they appear, you can counter with the truth - I AM PROSPEROUS.

# I WANNA BE RICH

By Reggie Calloway, Vincent Calloway,
Belinda Lipscomb and Melvin Arthur Gentry
Performed by Calloway

Cash, cold, that's what I need
Big bill collectors they ring my phone
They bother me when I'm not at home
Ain't go no time to be fooling round
Feet hit the floor, then I get head on down, you see

I want money lots and lots of money
I want the pie in the sky
I want money lots and lots of money
So don't be asking me why

I wanna be rich oh
I wanna be rich oh
I wanna be rich oh
I wanna be rich, full of love, peace and happiness

I want my cake wanna eat it too
I want the stars and the silver moon
I spend my money on lottery

My favourite number is 1 2 3, you see
Every way rich
Love, peace and happiness

# Worthy To Be Wealthy

I want all the things that lovers do
A pocket full of dreams come true
Even things you cannot find
Want you by my side to keep you satisfied and rich

Here is what we're gonna do
Say oh I say uh uh
Whoooaaa Whoaaaaa
Got to be baby
I just wanna to be rich
I just wanna be, just wanna be
Cause baby
I wanna be rich
You know what I mean baby
I wanna be rich

Everyday and every way
I wanna be rich, full of love, peace and happiness
Play, honey, there's lots and lots for everyone
Be rich, I wanna be rich

CHAPTER 10

# THE HEALING BALM OF
# WORTHINESS

There is something sacred that begins to unfold the moment you know—deep in your bones—that you are worthy. Not because of what you've done, not because of what you've overcome, and definitely not because you've checked off some imaginary list of accomplishments. No, this worthiness goes so much deeper. Soul-deep. It's the divine truth that's been waiting patiently for you to remember it.

When I began to truly know I was worthy—not just intellectually, but emotionally, spiritually, and viscerally—it was like light breaking through decades of darkness. And not just any light. It was healing, warm, forgiving light that found its way into the crevices of trauma that I had carried for far too long.

You see, trauma often teaches us the lie that something is wrong with us. That we deserved what happened. That we're broken, shameful, not enough. These lies take root in our subconscious and grow into belief systems—distorted frameworks that inform how we see ourselves and the world. They make us question our intuition, suppress our truth, and perform versions of ourselves just to feel safe.

But when we reclaim our worthiness, we reclaim our power.

Knowing you're worthy allows you to face trauma not with fear, but with compassion. You stop judging yourself for what you did to survive. You begin to see your coping mechanisms not as flaws, but as brilliant adaptations. And this shift changes everything. Worthiness dissolves shame. It silences the inner critic. It tells the nervous system, "You're safe now." And when your nervous system feels safe, healing becomes possible.

Worthiness invites you to tell yourself a new story—one rooted in love, not lack. It lets you revisit past pain not to relive it, but to release it. To honor what happened, yes, but more importantly, to stop allowing it to define who you are.

I've come to see that healing is not about fixing what's broken. It's about remembering what's whole. And worthiness is the bridge that helps you cross from survival into liberation. From self-doubt into authenticity. From trauma into truth.

When you know you're worthy, you no longer need to earn your healing. You simply allow it. You let the tears flow, the anger rise, the memories surface—not because you're broken, but because you're brave enough to feel what needs to be felt.

You're present enough to give the wounded parts of you the love they were always worthy of.

And as you do, something miraculous happens.

You soften. You open. You begin to trust yourself again. You begin to choose yourself—over and over, without apology.

That is the power of knowing you're worthy. It doesn't just inspire healing. It is healing. It is the homecoming your soul has been waiting for.

## Superpower of Your Worthiness

As you do the work to reconnect with your innate worth, there are other helpful tools to anchor your new awareness in your subconscious. In addition to affirming "I AM WORTHY" each day, engaging in fun activities that celebrate your worth facilitates the shift that allows you to align with and expand your worth consciousness.

Create a worthy playlist of songs that remind you that you're worthy. Following each chapter of this book are lyrics to some of my favorite songs. They certainly celebrate worthiness and I encourage you to add them to your playlist.

Frame one of your baby pictures or a photo of you at the youngest age available. Place it someplace conspicuous so that it's a daily reminder that you were born worthy.

Write a letter to your younger self. Choose an age that's significant and write a letter of gratitude thanking your younger self for being who they were; for accomplishing what she/he accomplished; for enduring what they endured; for surviving what they survived; for being who they were. You would not be the person you are now if they were not the person they were then.

You can literally change your life by becoming more intentional and attentional about this underrated internal quality that has been a part of you since you arrived on the planet. Your worthiness changes how you see yourself, removes your blind spots and smooths out how you move through the world. It's like a secret treasure chest within you that is bursting with manifesting power, but it is completely up to you to put the key in the lock and turn it.

# "THIS IS WHO I AM"
### Written and Performed by Celeste

Some flowers never get to bloom and see the days
Some flowers are content to wish their lives away
Some may rise, some may fall
But only you may see me true

So only you can tell them
This is who I am
This is who I am

You know me like a river knows how to flow
My body is a story you are always told
The sun may rise, the sun may fall
But only you may ever see me true
But only you can tell them
This is who I am
This is who I am

Send the white horses, seems I've exhausted
Those fickle games I play
Seen my good fortune made
But only you may see me true,
Only you can tell them this is who I am

This is who I am
This is who I am

This is who I am
THis is who I am
No lie, I'm no less

124

This is who I am
This is who I am
This is who I am
This is who I am
This is who I am
Sunrise to sunset
This is who I am

# THE WORTHY PRAYER

By Michelle Hollinger

I am worthy.
Just because I am.

No one else defines my worth.
No circumstance limits my worthiness.
I reclaim the power of my worthiness through forgiveness.

I am worthy.
Just because I am.

I am worthy of the very best life has to offer.
I am worthy of love, health, prosperity, peace and joy.
I unleash the energy of my worthiness and it shapes my
journey.

I am worthy.
Just because I am.

I am worthy of harmonious relationships.
And because they reflect the relationship I have with myself;
I honor me with love, compassion and respect.

I am worthy.
Just because I am.

Every day I embrace my worth.
I intentionally celebrate my worthiness.
I cherish my worth with thoughts, words and actions.

I am worthy. I use my voice.
I am worthy. My opinion matters.
I am worthy. I do not play small.
I am worthy. Settling is not an option.
I am worthy. I face my fear.

I am worthy.
Just because I am.

# BOOKS

*Key to Yourself*
Venice Bloodworth

*Spiritual Economics*
Eric Butterworth

*Thank and Grow Rich*
Pam Grout

*You Can Heal Your Life*
Louise Hay

*Think and Grow Rich*
Napoleon Hill

*Sis, You're Worth It*
Michelle Hollinger

*Radical Forgiveness*
Colin C. Tipping

# NEW THOUGHT SPIRITUAL CENTERS

Agape International
www.agapelive.com

Celebration Spiritual Center
www.celebrationsc.org

Universal Foundation for Better Living
www.ufbl.org

Unity Worldwide Ministries
www.unityworldwideministries.org

# ABOUT THE AUTHOR

Michelle Hollinger is a metaphysical New Thought student and an expert on worthiness. In 2020, Michelle established The Institute for Worthy Living, where she serves as president and Chief Worthiness Officer. The organization reminds people of their innate worth through workshops, retreats, innovative services and books. Learn more at www.theinstituteforworthyliving.com.

Michelle is the mother of three magnificent children, Alexandra, Stephanie and Tyler; the grandma of the amazing Naomi Michelle, the awesome Aaron Quinton and the mother in-love to the wonderful Jeremy Daniel.

Michelle is the author of *Sis, You're Worth It, The Sisterhood Exchange, Worthy* and *Are You Worthy? Powerful Steps for a Resounding Yes*, all available at your favorite bookstore.

A graduate of Florida State University, Michelle is a sociologist and a former social worker who authored two books for the child welfare industry, *The ABCs of Authentic Work with Families* and *Seven Steps to Strengthen Your Family.*

The founder and publisher of *The Sisterhood,* a magazine for women, Michelle is also the former editor of *The Miami Times* and the *South Florida Times*, two prominent Black newspapers.

She earned the master certificate from the Johnnie Colemon Theological Seminary and served as a prayer chaplain at Unity on the Bay and the Universal Truth Center. Ultimately, Michelle is on a mission to help people understand the power of their worthiness and how to use it as the superpower it is.

Learn more about her at www.michellehollinger.com and www.theinstituteforworthyliving.com.

# THANK YOU NOTE FROM MICHELLE:

Thank you for investing in your worthiness.
To go even deeper, I invite you to go to
https://1obtph4g.kartra.com/page/mIy2059
to download a free copy of the companion workbook for
Worthiness is Your Superpower.

Also, please feel free to reach out to me at
Michelle@theinstituteforworthyliving.com with questions,
comments, brilliant insights or success stories.

Peace,

**Michelle**

www.ingramcontent.com/pod-product-compliance
Lightning Source LLC
Chambersburg PA
CBHW052039150726
48002CB00002B/679